Simple Pleasures
OF
THE HOME

Cozy Comforts and Old-Fashioned Crafts
for Every Room in the House

Susannah Seton

CONARI PRESS
Berkeley, California

Conari Press books are distributed by Publishers Group West.

ISBN 1-57324-174-1

Cover illustration: Rae Ecklund
Cover and book design: Suzanne Albertson
Interior diagrams: Joan Carol
Interior illustrations: Rea Ecklund

The author wishes to gratefully acknowledge excerpts from: *Slowing Down in a Speeded Up World* by Adair Lara, ©1994 by Adair Lara, reprinted by permission of Conari Press; *Seasons of Aromatherapy* by Judith Fitzsimmons and Paula Bousquet, © 1999 by Judith Fitzsimmons and Paula Bousquet, reprinted by permission of Conari Press; *Goddess in the Kitchen* by Margie Lapanja, © 1998 by Margie Lapanja, reprinted by permission of Conari Press.

Library of Congress Cataloging-in-Publication Data

Seton, Susannah. 1952—
Simple pleasures of the home : cozy comforts and old-fashioned crafts for every room in the house / Susannah Seton.
p.   cm.
ISBN 1-57324-174-1
1. Handicraft.   2. Cookery.   I. Title.

TT157.S4159   1999   99-16034
745.5—dc21   CIP

Printed in the United States of America on recycled paper

99 00 01 02 03   Data Repro   10 9 8 7 6 5 4 3 2 1

There's no place
like home.

—Dorothy in *The Wizard of Oz*

Simple Pleasures
of the HOME

ACKNOWLEDGMENTS

Simple Pleasures of the Home is made up of a variety of voices who have generously shared their thoughts, feelings, and suggestions for making a house a home: Alicia Alvres, Ame Beanland, Yvonne and Bonnie Clark, Robin Demers, Heather Dever, Bill Edelstein, Cris Evatt, Shelly Glennon, Will Glennon, Nina Lesowitz, Ana Li, Laura Marceau, Nancy Margolis, Donald McIlraith, Barbara Parmet, Matthew Quincy, Mary Jane Ryan, Claudia Schaab, and Claudia Smelser. Thanks also to all the folks who work for Conari Press who made this book possible, both those mentioned above as well as Suzanne Albertson, Brenda Knight, Sharon Donovan, Everton Lopez, Annette Madden, Tom King, Pam Suwinsky, Marianne Dresser, and Teresa Coronado.

CONFESSIONS OF A HOMEBODY

> Ah! There is nothing like staying at
> home for real comfort.
>
> —JANE AUSTEN

Home. There are few words that carry such potent feelings. It's the place where we can let down our hair, loosen our clothes, put up our feet. It's where, often, those we love most share in the ordinariness and extraordinariness of our days—the birthdays and holidays, the blue Mondays and black Fridays, the everyday commonplace days. It's the place many of us long to run from, and others spent lifetimes trying to get back to. As the proverb goes, it's where our hearts are.

I love being at home. In fact, it's hard to blast me out of the house. Looking back at my life as a whole now that I'm in my forties, I realize I was bitten young by the domestic bug.

When I was a kid, I remember my brother and sister laughing at me because I didn't like to play outside like other kids. My homebodyness so concerned my mother that she'd occasionally lock me outside the house so I would get some fresh air and exercise. Often, particularly on snowy winter afternoons, I would sit at the front door, crying, until the time was up and I could come in again.

Mostly I wanted to be home so I could read, but reading wasn't my only home pleasure. I distinctly remember by age ten or so delighting in coming home to an empty house after school—mother off on errands, brother and sister not yet back from school. The solitude! The coziness of getting whatever I wanted to eat out of the fridge (usually lettuce with Wishbone Italian dressing—yes, I guess I was a bit of an odd bird) and then sitting at the dining room table or on the couch curled up in an afghan. Utter bliss.

I was the kind of kid who was at home learning from my mother how to make spaghetti sauce when the other kids were playing baseball. I loved making homemade cards for Christmas, birthdays, and other special occasions. I even liked cleaning the bathrooms and dusting as my chores (but I never did see the pleasure in vacuuming).

When I went away to college, I only spent a year in the dorms, quickly setting up the '70s equivalent of wedded bliss with a young man who enjoyed the domestic arts as much as I did. We loved to do laundry together during study breaks. Our idea of a good time was to concoct new ways to use Hamburger Helper—I recall a disastrous meal when we confused powered ginger with gingerroot. Unfortunately, we had to eat it for days on end because our food budget for the week had been used up. We used to grow our own sprouts and make our own yogurt. We potted plants and tended gardens. Cleaning up our room was always a great distraction from studying. We even illegally smuggled a kitten into student housing to make it feel more like home.

My instincts for creating a comfortable nest and sitting in it contentedly never left me. Not for me were wild nights on the town, months-long travels (I once lived for two months in a tent and that did it for me—I just wanted a place I could stand up in!), or a life of TV dinners on the run. No matter what my life circumstances have been—and they have varied wildly, from dirt poor to outright affluent—I've settled in with dozens of houseplants, thrown up a few pieces of artwork, and proceeded to needlepoint pillows, burn incense, and cook dinners from scratch every night. Even now, often I don't leave the house for days on end.

Don't get me wrong—I'm no Martha Stewart. I can't be bothered with visual perfection (which is fortunate since I have terrible fine motor coordination and can't wrap my fingers around half of the craft projects she dreams up), and I don't believe in making too much of a big deal about anything. I just love the basics of making and keeping a home—the cooking, cleaning, tidying, arranging, beautifying routine of it all.

That's why, in thinking about where I wanted to go next in the *Simple Pleasures* series, home was a natural for me—it has been through homemaking that I have experienced some of the greatest pleasures of my life. And so, once again, I asked people far and wide to share their stories, recipes, crafts, lotions, and other homespun creature comforts. The result is in your hands.

I'm a big proponent of simplicity in all the domestic arts—simple food, simple crafts, simple gifts and games for you and your family. In this and all my books, I advocate getting back to basics—appreciating the smell of freshly washed clothes, the bloom on your Christmas cactus, the feel of clean sheets. It is my belief that such simple pleasures surround us every day, and by tapping into them, we find joy in the ordinary, magic in the mundane. Particularly when it comes to homemaking, all of us, no matter how domestically challenged, spend a great deal of our lives on these routine tasks of life—cooking, cleaning, and the like. So we might as well get the maximum satisfaction from them.

That's why, no matter where you call home, it is my fervent wish that *Simple Pleasures of the Home* will help you connect to the heart of your home, to what truly matters to you in your daily life. For the more we all live from our hearts, the more gracious and beautiful the world will be when we venture past our own doorsteps.

THE KITCHEN

The whole of nature, as has been said,
is a conjugation of the verb to eat,
in the active and passive.

—WILLIAM RALPH INGE

Breaking the Fast

I love breakfast. Always have. I love all the traditional breakfast items—orange juice, waffles, pancakes, eggs, bacon, bagels, coffee. My favorite thing on a Sunday morning is to wake up late and, still in pajamas, make a leisurely breakfast—a goat cheese omelet, perhaps, with Kalamata olives and sundried tomatoes—and spread out over the kitchen table with the *New York Times*. Sometimes I can make breakfast last till 2 P.M. What a joy!

Raisin Scones

Scones are becoming increasingly popular breakfast items. They're easy to make, and because these are made with oats, they have the added benefit of being good for you.

⅓ cup butter or margarine, melted

⅓ cup milk

1 egg, beaten

1½ cups flour

¼ cup sugar

1 tablespoon baking powder

¹/₄ teaspoon salt

¹/₄ teaspoon cream of tartar

1¹/₄ cups quick oats

¹/₃ cup raisins

Combine butter or margarine with milk and egg in a large bowl. Set aside. Sift together flour, sugar, baking powder, salt, and cream of tartar. Add gradually to milk mixture, stirring well. Add oats and raisins and mix well.

Preheat oven to 400° F. With flour-coated hands, form the dough into an 8-inch circle on a lightly floured cookie sheet. Cut into 8 wedges. Separate wedges slightly and bake for 12–15 minutes or until lightly browned. Makes 8.

Baking Bread

I've been scanning the sales ads, thinking about getting a bread machine. Maybe if I wait awhile, I think, I can get one cheaper. But then I remember how I like to smack the dough to see if it's kneaded enough—as one book said, it should feel like a baby's bottom. That thought reminds me how connected I feel to countless generations of women who have made bread for their families, and how much I love the smell of bread baking.

I wonder how it would feel for that bread to come from a machine into which I dump ingredients in the rush of doing something else, then punch in the correct time-delay sequence. No more thinking of all the women who have made bread before me; no more smacking it to see if it feels like a baby's bottom.

On second thought, I think I'll keep the flour on the floor, the overactive yeast oozing out of the cup, and the awkward tiptoe position I have to assume to knead the bread on a counter that's too high. I'll keep it all, happily.

> *Bread deals with living things, with giving life,*
> *with growth, with the seed, the grain that*
> *nurtures. It is not coincidence that we*
> *say bread is the staff of life.*
> —LIONEL POILANE

Basic White Bread

Nothing beats the smell of bread baking in the oven or the warm loaves sitting on the counter. It creates such a feeling of home! Here's a basic recipe.

1¼ cups low-fat milk, scalded

1½ tablespoons honey

1¼ teaspoons salt

2 tablespoons canola, corn, or safflower oil, plus a bit more

1¼-ounce package dry yeast

¼ cup warm water (105–115° F)

3⅓ cups unbleached flour, approximately

Combine the first four ingredients in a large bowl. Stir and let cool to lukewarm. In a small bowl, dissolve yeast in warm water and add to milk mixture. Add flour to mixture, a little bit at a time, to form a stiff dough. Mix well after each addition. Turn onto a lightly floured board and knead until smooth and elastic.

Grease a large bowl and add dough, turning dough to grease all sides. Cover with a damp towel and let rise in a warm place until double in size. Punch down and let rest until double in size again. Punch down and let rest for 10 minutes. Preheat oven to 375° F. Shape dough into a loaf and place in a greased 9-by-5-by-3-inch bread pan. Brush top with oil. Cover and let rise until double in size.

Bake loaf until done, about 40 minutes. It should be brown on top and sound hollow when struck. Makes 1 loaf.

The smell of new bread is comfortable to
the head and to the heart.
—Anonymous, circa 1400s

Herbal Bouquet

When I purchase fresh herbs or gather them from my garden, I like to cut off the bottoms and place them in a nice vase on my kitchen windowsill. This not only brightens up the kitchen, it adds fragrance, keeps the herbs fresher longer, and has the added benefit of reminding me to use them in a variety of dishes.

Cutting Capers

There is nothing, I repeat nothing, that beats the feeling of cutting with a truly sharp knife. The satisfying whack to halve an onion, then a rapid chopping to mince it perfectly; slicing through beef as if it were butter; actually cutting rather than mushing a tomato—preparing food is a true pleasure provided the knives are sharp enough. I'm such a fanatic about knives that my husband even bought a whetstone; when things get a bit too dull, he carts it out and sharpens things up again.

Paint with Passion

My kitchen is tiny (roughly 4-by-8-feet) and was rather unattractive when I moved in. I decided to add character to it by painting the trim an unconventional color. Years back, I had clipped a photo of what I thought was an incredibly beautiful kitchen and had saved it in a folder with some other decorating ideas. What I most liked about the kitchen in the photo was the unusual green that was used on the trim. My kitchen was so ugly that I had nowhere to go but up, so I was open to just about anything. When I first applied the green paint, it was pretty shocking—it was the color of comic book kryptonite—even though it had looked "perfect" at Kelly-Moore. I toned it down with some beige paint that I had on hand, and it came out just right. I love looking at it.

Taking the Plunge

If you are inspired to go wild with trim, consider the following suggestions:

1. Stay away from trendy colors—you're probably going to be living with that room for a long time. Plus, you might just want something different than what everyone else has.

2. Don't be afraid to mess up—you can always paint over it.

3. Think about the surrounding accent colors—will what you have mesh with the new color you've chosen?

"Roast Beef, Medium" is not only a food.
It is a philosophy.
—EDNA FERBER

Mindful Eating

I used to be a remarkably fast eater, and I read or watched TV while eating. I still do that during some meals. On most days, though, I eat my breakfast cereal very slowly and remember to bow to the bowl before each spoonful. Also, I bow to my water glass before each drink. I try to make the bow a slow one: I try to hold it for a beat and then breathe slowly and deeply when coming out of it.

During that bow and while eating, I try to think of all the sacrifices and hard work that have gone into making this food. I try to visualize the farms in Iowa and orchards in California where it was grown, the people working there and what exactly they do, the clerks who put it on the store shelves, the clerk who sold it to me. I think about what I will do with the life the food gives me.

Dish Delight

Some women want their husbands to help do dishes after the evening meal. I only want my husband to bring the dishes over from the table, then he can be on his way to watch TV or read the paper, because the next half-hour or forty-five minutes are all mine. Yes, I have a dishwasher, but while I wash the pots and pans or clean the stove top and counters, I'm collecting my thoughts, thinking through troubling problems, brainstorming ideas for a short story, or just letting my mind wander.

Let the dishes be few in number,
but exquisitely chosen.
—ANTHELME BRILLAT-SAVARIN

Cooking with Kids

I'm a great believer in getting kids into the kitchen as early as possible. Even little kids, with help, can do things such as stir and mix ingredients (but not on the stove), mash potatoes, turn pasta makers, or decorate cookies. Later they can graduate to making cinnamon toast and other treats kids crave. By ten they should be able to construct whole meals, if the meals are simple enough.

I taught my twelve-year-old stepson to cook by assigning him a dinner per week. He was in charge of picking the menu and putting it together. I was around for support—showing him how to hold an onion so he wouldn't chop his fingers off when cutting, reminding him that pasta should cook with the lid off, rice with it on. I really enjoyed passing on my expertise, and he (usually) enjoyed the responsibility and sense of satisfaction he got when we all devoured his creations.

There is a charm in improvised eating which
a regular meal lacks.
—GRAHAM GREENE

Rock Candy

Remember this old-fashioned candy? It's a great kid-friendly cooking project.

1 cup sugar

1 cup water

1 teaspoon vanilla, peppermint, or other flavoring, optional

wooden skewers about 3 inches long

small wide-necked glass bottles or jars such as those that apple
 juice comes in

food coloring

aluminum foil

Boil water and sugar until sugar is completely dissolved.
Add flavoring if desired. Pour into bottles or jars and add
food coloring, stirring with a wooden skewer. Cover each jar
with foil, then poke a wooden skewer through the foil into
each jar. Let sit until sugar-water has cooled and crystals have
formed. Voilà! Rock candy. Makes 1 cup—quantity varies
depending on number of jars.

A Great Meal

I can't cook. Because I'm a woman and "supposed" to know how, I've decided to be horrible at it. Some weekends, though, I'm overcome by the desire to prepare a meal. A great meal.

I take all day. I imagine what the perfect meal would be—fresh, organic vegetables, wonderfully ripe fruit, a beautiful salad, maybe a light pasta, some freshly caught seafood . . . whatever. Then I plan my route. My favorite cheese shop is always a stop: I'll ask the man at the counter, "What do you recommend?" He'll give me a taste of a new cheese from Denmark or Provence that makes me swoon, and I'll buy it.

Next I stop by the bakery. Usually a baguette is the perfect accouterment to go with my cheese, and right on the spot I eat part of it to get me through the rest of my strenuous day. Then I go to my favorite corner produce stand and the health food store. I load up on veggies and fruit, imagining all of the salads and succulent fruits that I'll dine on. And finally I stop and buy a bottle of wine. A good merlot.

When I get home, I unpack my groceries. I open the wine. I slice up my baguette and spread on the ripe cheese. I cut up my cantaloupe and garnish it with strawberries and purple grapes. The little organic pear-shaped tomatoes, along with an avocado, are thrown onto some crisp lettuce and lightly mist-ed with oil and vinegar, salt and pepper. And then I take my delectables to the kitchen table, where my favorite book is waiting, and I eat.

Stock Delight

For me, the delight of making soup stock is in the act of chopping and skimming, the kitchen windows steaming up, and the room filling with the scent of chicken bones, the whole heads of garlic, great lifeboats of carrots, onions, and celery, and a gauze purse filled with parsley, black peppercorns, bay leaves, dried thyme, and oregano and tied up with string—the mysterious bouquet garni.

My result is an essential product, but the real benefit is time engaged with myself. Only a small part of my mind is occupied, and the rest is free to wander where it will. It is the last bastion, as my back injury has wiped out my former activities: woolgathering, gardening, running, and long drives. They all required some kind of intact frame, and I am a rickety old scaffolding that collapses with the slightest breeze. Instead, I have miniaturized my sense of wonder and have come to appreciate the glories of well-made stock and things that come to fruition slowly and lovingly.

Eating is heaven.
—KOREAN PROVERB

Crazy for Crackers

When I'm working at home, I get the munchies something fierce. It's probably a desire for a distraction from writing. Since I don't want to load up on calories, I've taken to eating crackers—sometimes plain, often with salsa or, if I am feeling particularly naughty, lower-fat cheddar cheese. Recently I came across a recipe for homemade crackers. To my delight, I found that they are incredibly easy to make and much better than any store-bought ones. I love sesame seeds, so I sprinkle some on just before baking—you can too!

Homemade Crackers

2 cups all-purpose flour

1 teaspoon baking powder

pinch of salt

4 tablespoons butter, margarine, or shortening

¾ cup water, approximately

sesame seeds, optional

Preheat oven to 325° F. Sift together flour, baking powder, and salt. With two knives, cut the shortening into the flour until mixture is fine. Add just enough water to make a firm dough. On a lightly floured surface, with a floured rolling pin, thinly roll out the dough. Using a round cookie cutter, stamp out crackers; prick them all over with a fork, and sprinkle with salt and sesame seeds if desired. Bake on a lightly greased cookie sheet for 20 minutes or until crisp. Cool on a rack and store in an airtight container. Makes 2 dozen.

> *Cooking is at once one of the simplest and most*
> *gratifying of the arts, but to cook well, one*
> *must love and respect food.*
> —CRAIG CLAIBORNE

Newfound Pleasure

I can't cook—or at least I'm late in learning. I come from the generation of men who were instructed to stay out of the kitchen, and so I mostly have for the past sixty years (barbecuing is a different story—that was my turf). But when I retired, I had a lot of time on my hands and, with my wife at work all day, I just found myself drifting into the kitchen. First I tried my hand at sourdough bread made with starter that my daughter in San Francisco sent. I did that every week for a year or so. Then I moved onto what I called "Healthy Breakfast Muffins"—a combination of whole wheat, oat bran, raisins, etc. On Sunday evenings I would make enough to last the week. Heavy, but good for you. But my pièce de résistance, the apogee of my culinary ability, is seafood chowder. I created it one day when my wife was going to be late from work and I thought I would surprise her with dinner on the table. I did— and I surprised myself; it was that good.

Seafood Chowder

You can make this with low-fat milk, regular milk, or cream. The richer the liquid, the more delectable the taste (but the higher the fat content). You can also substitute olive oil for the bacon (use 1 tablespoon oil to cook the onion in), but again, it won't taste as good.

  ¼ pound bacon, diced

  1 medium onion, chopped

  3 cups water or fish stock

  3 medium potatoes, diced

  1 carrot, grated

  1 celery, diced

  2 pounds boneless fish such as cod, cut into bite-sized pieces

  4 cups milk or heavy cream

  2 tablespoons chopped parsley or chives

Place the bacon in a large soup pot on medium-high heat until it begins to get crisp. Add the chopped onion and cook until wilted, about 5 minutes. Add water or stock, potatoes, carrot, and celery. Simmer until potatoes are tender, about 10 minutes. Add fish and simmer until just cooked through, 1 or 2 minutes. Add the milk and parsley or chives and simmer until heated through. Serves 4.

No Bake Zone

I love to cook but I hate baking. I don't know why that is, but I am not a dessert chef. I've perfected the art of suggesting a dessert when someone asks what he or she can bring for dinner, and I have a wide selection of no-baking desserts— poached fruit in winter, fruit salads in summer. Here's one that's always been a crowd-pleaser.

Watermelon Basket

To make this nonalcoholic, substitute orange juice for the sherry.

1 small watermelon

2 cantaloupes

½ pound seedless grapes

1 cup sherry

3 tablespoons fresh mint, chopped

1 pound peaches

In the morning, cut watermelon in half lengthwise and remove fruit with a melon scoop. Cover the watermelon shell and refrigerate it. With the melon scoop, remove fruit from cantaloupes and combine with watermelon and grapes in a large bowl. Add the sherry and mint and mix well. Refrigerate at least 6 hours. Just before serving, slice the peaches, combine with the rest of the fruit, and place in the watermelon shell. Serves 12.

> *Cooking is ... sculpture of the soul. A good cook works by the fire of the imagination, not merely by the ... fire in the stove.*
> —ROBERT TRISTRAM COFFIN

Gifts from the Garden

My husband and I are avid gardeners—he does the vegetables, I do the flowers. But when it comes to harvest time, we both get into the act, canning, jamming, and drying. We make lots of tomato sauce, sundried tomatoes in oil, plum jam, garlic braids, and homegrown dried spice mixes. Some we use for ourselves, but most we give away as holiday gifts. Our friends have come to expect their annual allotment of these treats, and if we have a bad year and have to cut back, we always hear about it. Recently we have been winning raves for our flavored vinegars. We have created some unusual combinations that people really love. Here's one.

Cranberry Vinegar

You've heard of raspberry vinegar, but how about cranberry vinegar? It's great on holiday salads and chicken dishes.

    1 cup fresh cranberries per 1 quart white wine vinegar

Wash and pick over the cranberries; dry well on paper towels. Pack the cranberries into clean bottles or jars with lids or corks, and fill with vinegar that has been heated just to the boiling point. Cork or cap the jars and stand them on a sunny windowsill for about 2 weeks (4 weeks if not very sunny). The warmth of the sun will infuse the vinegar with the cranberry flavor. Taste test—if it doesn't seem flavorful enough, strain the vinegar and add more cranberries to it. When it suits you, label and decorate the jars with a beautiful ribbon. Store at room temperature.

Low-Fat Challenge

Recently I have become concerned about my cholesterol and have had to change the way I've been eating. At first I hated it—all I could think about was all the cheese, butter, beef, and potato chips I was missing. But then I decided to try and enjoy the challenge of learning to cook in a new way and the pleasure of adapting and experimenting in the kitchen to come up with low-fat meals my family and I would like. It's working. I'm actually enjoying myself—and losing weight and lowering my cholesterol in the process. I've learned a few tricks I'd like to share:

Tricks for Low-Fat Cooking

- Rather than sautéing onions in butter or oil, braise them in wine, broth, or water over medium heat. The onions cook as the liquid boils off. Red wine is great for any tomato-based sauces using onions.

- Steam, broil, or grill rather than bake or fry. For example, if you have a recipe calling for eggplant fried in oil, broil or grill it instead.

- Use vegetable oil spray (there are even sprayers for olive oil at kitchen supply stores now). Spraying uses a lot less oil than if you were to pour it on.

- Get good nonstick pans. These allow you to sauté on high with little or no oil.

- Experiment with replacing full-fat dairy products with low-fat or non-fat ones—for example, non-fat yogurt in Stroganoff or non-fat evaporated milk in pumpkin pies. (A word of caution: Usually the low-fat items replace beautifully with no adaptations needed. The non-fat options are trickier: for example, non-fat cheeses do not bake well, and you should heat non-fat yogurt very gently over low heat to prevent separation.)

- Depending on the recipe, substitute boneless, skinless, chicken breasts for beef or lamb. This works great in kebabs, Stroganoff, and chili.

- Marinate meat in oil-less marinades. I just eliminate the oil in recipes for marinades and have yet to find one that docsn't work without the oil.

> *What love is to the heart, appetite is to the stomach. The stomach is the conductor that leads and livens up the great orchestra of our emotions.*
> —GIOACCHINO ROSSINI

Patriotic Chicken

This chicken is a low-fat entrée—provided you remove the skin when eating.

4 chicken breast halves, with skin on

   salt and pepper to taste

2 cups fresh raspberries and blueberries, mixed

2 tablespoons chives, chopped

1 onion, sliced

Rinse the chicken and pat dry. Create a pocket in each by loosening the skin with your fingers. Salt and pepper the chicken and set aside.

In a food processor or a blender, purée 1 cup berries. Pour over the chicken, sprinkle the chives on top, cover, and refrigerate for several hours.

Preheat oven to 350° F. Remove the chicken from the marinade and place in a greased baking dish. Discard the marinade. In the pocket you have created in each breast, stuff ¼ cup berries and a quarter of the onion. Bake until the juices run clear when cut, about 45 minutes. Serves 4.

Handmade Pretzels

Pretzels are great non-fat snacks which can easily be made at home. The longer you knead, the softer the pretzel will be. If you've got kids, enlist them; to make it more fun, the dough can easily be formed in the shapes of letters and numbers.

1½ cups warm water

1 package yeast

1 tablespoon sugar

4 cups flour

1 teaspoon salt, plus more for tops

1 egg, beaten

Preheat oven to 425° F. In a large bowl, dissolve yeast in

warm water. Add sugar, flour, and salt. Mix well, then knead dough until it is smooth and soft. Roll and twist dough into desired shapes—letters, numbers, twists, etc. Lay the pretzel dough shapes onto two greased cookie sheets. Brush with beaten egg and sprinkle lightly with salt. Bake for 12–15 minutes or until golden. Makes 1–2 dozen, depending on size.

Hearty Food

I try to eat healthy and minimize my meat consumption. But some Sundays, when the weather turns cold, I start to crave an old-fashioned, hearty meal—like a pot roast with mashed potatoes or corned beef and cabbage. A stick-to-your-ribs kind of dinner like my mom used to make. I take out the box of old recipe cards my mother gave me of her favorite dishes, and riffle through them, looking for the thing that will just hit the spot. I know that I've found the right recipe when my mouth starts to water. I run to the store for the ingredients and spend the afternoon making the dish that will indulge my craving. No matter what it turns out to be, my kids call it "Mom's Missing Grandma" dish.

> *The angels in Paradise eat nothing but*
> *vermicelli al pomodoro.*
> —MAYOR OF NAPLES, 1930

Rolled Beef

Here's one of those hearty favorites. It's a takeoff on the German dish sauerbraten. Very delicious, particularly with mashed potatoes.

1 3–4 pound beef round roast, trimmed

1/4 cup Dijon mustard

1/2 pound bacon, sliced in half

2 medium onions, 1 chopped, 1 quartered

1 8-ounce jar dill pickles, thinly sliced lengthwise

1 quart plus 1/4 cup water

1 28-ounce can whole tomatoes, crushed

4 bay leaves

5 bouillon cubes

1/2 cup corn starch

Turn roast lengthwise and slice into 1/4-inch slices approximately 6 inches long by 4 inches wide. Place beef slices, one by one, between sheets of waxed paper and pound with a rolling pin to flatten. Do not puncture.

Spread each slice with 1 teaspoon mustard. Place a half slice of bacon, 1 tablespoon chopped onion, and 2 pickle slices on each beef slice. Roll meat up and secure with toothpicks or string.

Place meat in a Dutch oven and brown on all sides. Add 1 quart water and let simmer, uncovered, for 1 hour. Add tomatoes, quartered onion, bay leaves, and bouillon cubes.

Cover and simmer for another hour.

Remove meat from pan. Set aside. Strain liquid and discard solids. Return liquid to pan and bring to boil.

In a small bowl, combine cornstarch and ¼ cup cold water. Add to liquid to thicken. Reduce heat to simmer and return meat to pan. Simmer for 1 hour. Serves 8.

Braendende Kaelighted

This is Danish comfort food, designed to dispel the gloom of winter. Its name means "burning love." Fat-phobics, beware!

> 1 pound of potatoes, peeled and cut into chunks
> 8–10 slices bacon, chopped
> 3 onions, chopped
> 4 tablespoons butter
> ½ pint cream (can substitute milk or low-fat milk)
> salt, pepper, and nutmeg to taste

Cook potatoes in water until tender. While potatoes are cooking, fry bacon with onions until onions are tender. Drain potatoes and mash. Whip in butter and cream or milk. Season with spices.

Mound potatoes on a plate and make a well in the center. Place bacon-onion mixture in the center. Serves 4.

The Smell of Happiness

For me, there is nothing like a well-brewed cup of coffee in the morning. The aroma that greets me as I enter the kitchen is what I live for when I get up every morning. I prepare my coffee maker the night before so that the timer is set for 5 minutes before my alarm goes off. When my eyes open, I can already smell the faint scent of satisfaction. I stumble to the kitchen, get out my special mug, pour, and imbibe. Ah!

Pie Love

I love baking pies: pumpkin, apple, blackberry. There's nothing that compares to a luscious fruit pie still warm from the oven and smothered with vanilla ice cream. That's my idea of heaven. Since my time is limited, I do cheat a bit and buy a frozen crust (Nancy's Deep Dish from Safeway is my favorite). But if you don't say anything, no one else has to know. Here's a recipe that has been a favorite of mine—and my guests— through the years.

Rosy Apple Pie

¾ cup sugar

½ cup water

¼ cup red cinnamon candies (Red-Hots)

5 medium cooking apples (about 5 cups apple slices)

1 tablespoon flour

1 teaspoon lemon juice

1 tablespoon butter or margarine

9-inch double pie crust

Preheat oven to 400° F. In a medium saucepan, combine sugar, water, and cinnamon candies; cook until candies dissolve. Pare, core, and slice apples. Add to sugar mixture and simmer until apples are red. Drain; save syrup. Blend flour into cooled syrup and add lemon juice. Spread apples in a pastry-lined 9-inch pie plate and pour syrup over apples. Dot with butter. Cover with top crust, seal, and flute edges. Cut slits for escape of steam. Bake about 30 minutes until desired brownness. Makes 1 pie.

A Victorious Battle

The only time that I really feel a deep need to clean a place is when I first move into a new home, when I have been absent for a while, or when guests move out—it is a way of (re)claiming the space for myself. I particularly enjoy tackling the kitchen— the stove top, sink, cupboards, refrigerator, and, if I feel particularly energetic, the oven. I wipe and scrub, swipe and tidy.

What a sense of satisfaction to make it sparkle and shine! I even find myself examining my work after I'm done as a conqueror would survey his territory after a victorious battle.

Personalized Refrigerator Magnets

Can you ever have enough kitchen magnets? With all that I try to tack up there, I certainly can't. Here's an easy way to make your own (and they're great gifts for Grandma that kids can make themselves.)

Save the metal lids from frozen drink cans when you open them. Take some favorite photos that will fit on the lids and have color copies made. Cut the pictures to fit and, using white glue or spray glue, fix them to the lids, smoothing out any bubbles or wrinkles with your fingers. Glue a thin piece of ribbing around the edge and a magnet on the back. Presto!

Peach-Pear Fruit Leather

My daughter adores fruit rolls. And they can be very pricey, particularly the organic kind I buy. So I decided to roll up my sleeves and do my own. It's incredibly easy—and you can easily double or triple the recipe.

2 cups peaches, washed, peeled, pitted, and halved
2 cups pears, washed, peeled, halved, and cored

1–2 tablespoons honey or corn syrup

½ teaspoon lemon juice

Cut fruit into 1-inch chunks and purée in a blender or food processor together with the lemon juice. Add the honey, 1 tablespoon for each 1–2 cups of purée, depending on the tartness of the fruit.

If using a dehydrator, pour the purée gently on dehydrator trays lined with plastic wrap (scotch tape plastic on the bottom of the tray so plastic doesn't curl over the purée). Spread out evenly almost to the edge of the tray. Put the tray immediately into the dehydrating unit. Check the leather at least 6–8 hours after starting the drying process. Touch the middle to see if it is dry to the touch or still spongy. When the spongy spots are nearly gone and the edges look dry, free the plastic wrap from the tray, turn the leather upside down, peel the plastic wrap off the back, and return the leather to the dehydrator. An hour or two later, the back side should be dried.

If using an oven, spread the purée on a cookie sheet and place in a 130° F oven. Check after 4 hours; when edges look dry, turn over with a spatula and dry other side. The whole process should take about 6 hours. You can also dry fruit leather in the sun. Depending on the day, it could take as little as 8 hours.

After the leather is completely dried and cool, cut to the size you wish and roll up in plastic wrap for storage in a cool, dry, dark spot. Keeps well for 6 months to a year. Makes approximately 10 servings.

The Delights of Virtual Cooking

If you are a great peruser of recipes, check out the website **www.kitchenlink.com**. It has an exhaustive listing of recipes and food-related information. What I like about it is that you can type in a key word—let's say you have an abundance of broccoli and are looking for something different to do with it—and up pops a slew of recipes. Looking for low-fat and low-cal dishes? Check out **www.fatfree.com** and **www.cyberdiet.com**. If you are looking for a good place to buy natural food, don't miss Good Eats Shop-At-Home Natural Foods at **www.goodeats.com**. And over 6,000 recipes are available at **www.epicurious.com**, while **www.foodchannel.com** will link you to cooking contests, games, and restaurant reviews.

The purpose of a cookery book is unmistakable.
Its object can conceivably be no other than to
increase the happiness of mankind.
—JOSEPH CONRAD

Rosemary Wreath

Rosemary is something that grows in abundance in many parts of the country. And I love to use it fresh. So I've learned to make this simple rosemary heart to hang in my kitchen. I just tear off sprigs as I need them. If I don't use it fast enough, no problem—it's just as tasty dry.

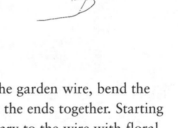

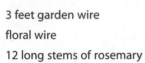

3 feet garden wire

floral wire

12 long stems of rosemary

Make a hook at each end of the garden wire, bend the wire into a heart shape, and hook the ends together. Starting at the top, attach a stem of rosemary to the wire with floral wire so that its leafy top points into the middle.

Repeat on other side, then wire stems down both sides and join at the bottom. Makes 1 wreath.

Comfort Food

Comfort food is anything simple that makes you feel good when you eat it. Many people's favorites tend to be somewhat bland, white, and harken back to childhood—mashed potatoes, macaroni and cheese, cinnamon toast on white bread, vanilla ice cream. But whatever makes your heart go pitter-patter culinarily is, to my mind, comfort food—mine happens to be kosher baby dill pickles, but chocolate has an awful lot of takers. After an informal poll of friends and family, I have collected six recipes of the top vote-getters in the comfort food department. May they bring you great joy!

> *My idea of heaven is a great big baked potato*
> *and someone to share it with.*
> —OPRAH WINFREY

Baking Powder Biscuits

Here is a real blast from the past. They've been out of favor so long that chic breakfast places are making a name for themselves by bringing them back into vogue. They're absolutely fabulous with butter and honey or raspberry jam.

1¾ cups all-purpose flour

½ teaspoon salt

3 teaspoons baking powder

5 tablespoons butter or other shortening

1 cup milk

Preheat oven to 450° F. Sift flour, salt, and baking powder into a large bowl. Using two knives, cut the shortening into the flour until the mixture resembles coarse cornmeal. Make a well in the center and add the milk. Stir for 1 minute, then drop from a spoon onto an ungreased cookie sheet. Bake for 12–14 minutes or until lightly browned. Makes 24 1½-inch biscuits.

> *Why has our poetry eschewed*
> *The rapture and response of food?*
> *What hymns are sung,*
> *What praises said*
> *For homemade miracles of bread?*
> —LOUIS UNTERMEYER

Pickled Eggs

Don't knock 'em till you've tried 'em. Friends swear by these.

12 eggs
1 quart white vinegar
6 cloves garlic, peeled
1 tablespoon peppercorns
1 tablespoon allspice berries
1 ounce sliced gingerroot

Cook the eggs in simmering water for 10 minutes; allow to cool completely, then peel. Combine vinegar with remaining ingredients and let simmer for 10 minutes. Pack the eggs into canning jars and pour the vinegar-spice mixture over the eggs so they are covered completely and there is a half-inch of head room. Put lids on tightly and process in a pan of boiling water for 10 minutes, making sure the water is covering the jars by 2 inches. Leave to cool. Check the seals and place the jars in a cool, dry spot. The eggs can be eaten after 1 month.

Celery Seed Coleslaw

We vinegar fans love this sweet-and-sour coleslaw recipe—it uses vinegar, not mayonnaise, to bind it.

½ cup sugar

½ cup cider vinegar

1 teaspoon celery seeds

½ teaspoon turmeric

1 teaspoon salt

3 tablespoons vegetable oil

3 tablespoons water

2 pounds cabbage, shredded

1 onion, grated

Combine all ingredients except cabbage and onion in a saucepan. Bring to a boil and simmer until sugar dissolves, about 2–3 minutes. Remove from heat and let cool. Combine cabbage and onion in a large bowl and add dressing. Cover and refrigerate overnight. Serves 8.

Old-Fashioned Egg Cream

Contrary to popular belief, there were never eggs in egg creams. The name came from the fact that its taste is as rich as eggs. You really need the large fountain glasses to do this right.

2 tablespoons chocolate syrup

¹/₃ cup milk

²/₃ cup cold seltzer water

Place the syrup in a glass. Add the milk and stir until blended. Add seltzer, stir, and serve. Makes 1 cup.

Rice Pudding

Rice pudding is really a love-or-hate thing—those who love it can't live without it. Others will pass, thank you.

1 cup long-grain white rice

2 cups water

1 teaspoon salt

³/₄ cup sugar

3 cups milk

3 egg yolks

2 teaspoons vanilla

¹/₂ cup raisins, soaked in water and drained

cinnamon

Combine rice, water, and salt in a medium saucepan and

simmer for 3 minutes. Add sugar and 2 cups milk and simmer, uncovered, over low heat, stirring occasionally to prevent scorching. Cook until rice is tender, about 20 minutes. Cool.

Preheat oven to 300° F. Grease a 1½-quart baking dish. Whisk the egg yolks with the vanilla and remaining 1 cup milk. Add raisins. Pour into baking dish, sprinkle with cinnamon, and bake, uncovered, until set at edges and creamy at center, about 20–25 minutes. Serves 4.

Chocolate Pudding

There is nothing like real chocolate pudding made from scratch! It's actually quite simple. If you are a fan of the "skin" of the pudding, chill uncovered (and chill longer—the more you wait, the thicker it will get). If you dislike it, cover tightly and serve as soon as it's cold.

    4 tablespoons cocoa
    4 tablespoons cornstarch
    ⅔ cup sugar
    ¼ teaspoon salt
    2 cups light cream
    1 teaspoon vanilla

In the top of a double boiler over hot but not boiling water, combine cocoa, cornstarch, sugar, and salt. Add ½ cup cream and stir until smooth. Stir remaining cream in slowly and constantly until thick. Stir in vanilla. Pour into container and chill. Serves 4.

> *Research tells us that fourteen out of any ten*
> *individuals like chocolate.*
> —SANDRA BOYNTON

The Nose Knows

What can compare to the smell of home cooking as you walk in the door after a hard day's work? I like it so much that I've taken to Crock-Pot cooking when it's my night to cook so that the aromas will be awaiting me when I come in the kitchen doorway.

Don't Forget the Dimmer

Why is it that when people are installing dimmers, they always remember the bedroom, the dining room, and the living room but ignore the kitchen? Whenever I move, putting a dimmer in the kitchen is my first priority. That way when guests come over and gather in the kitchen, as they invariably will, the lighting is as soft and flattering as the rest of the house.

Mass Production Cooking

I love to gather a group of people to make something that is best done in an assembly line—Christmas cookies or tamales, for example. I buy all the ingredients, invite over neighbors or friends, open a bottle of wine, and cook, cook, cook. The time speeds by, the work goes quickly, and everyone goes home with a big pile of whatever we've made that afternoon. As far as I'm concerned, it's the perfect blend of conviviality and cuisine.

The Bedroom

Only one hour in the normal day is more
pleasurable than the hour spent in bed with a
book before going to sleep, and that is the hour
spent in bed with a book after being
called in the morning.

—Rose Macaulay

Clean Sheets

I absolutely love the feel of clean sheets on the bed. It's a real treat for my Saturday nights. I do the laundry on Saturday, and when I put the clean sheets on the bed, I can already smell the freshness and feel the sensation on my skin. Such a little thing—and so satisfying.

Connecting to Heritage

Every so often, more when I was little, I'll spend an afternoon rummaging through my mother's dressers. Not through her private things, but through all the family things—my grand-mother's glove box, the box of old lace, those improbable baby christening dresses, the fans (black ostrich feathers, woodcuts, a leather traveling fan), her ivory silk brocade shawl, and of course the jewelry—my mother's gaudy '60s costume jewelry, my grandfather's Masonic watch fob, my great-grandmother's rings. Playing with these things, visiting them—because of course I have to try on all the gloves and open all the fans—reminds me that I have a past.

> *I will make you brooches and toys for your delight*
> *Of birdsong at morning and starshine at night.*
>
> —ROBERT LOUIS STEVENSON

Beautiful Boxes

I have a secret pleasure. It's making the insides of my drawers and closets beautiful. No one ever sees them except me—and that's what gives me the thrill. Even the cleaning supply drawer is attractively organized. But where I really go to town is in my bedroom closet. I keep all my small items—jewelry, stockings, hair ribbons—as well as my hats in beautiful rose-covered boxes that I have found or made over the years. Some are fabric covered, others are wallpapered, but they all share the romantic rose and ribbons of Victorian yesteryear. Sometimes when I'm home alone, I open the closet, lie in bed, and look at the soft colors and smile to myself over the absolute tidiness of it all.

Handmade Bandboxes

In the Victorian era, such boxes were called bandboxes, smaller versions of ladys' hatboxes. You can make your own very easily by keeping your eye out for interestingly shaped cardboard boxes with loose-fitting lids (so they will close when the fabric is added). But even an old shoe box will do quite nicely, as will a heart-shaped candy box.

1 cardboard box with loose-fitting lid

lightweight fabric, wallpaper, or wrapping paper of
  your choice

spray glue for paper, fabric glue for fabric

Place paper or fabric on the top of the lid and measure to fit, leaving 1 inch on each side to allow for overlap. Do the same for the sides of the box.

Cover the sides of the box with fabric or paper, using a light coat of appropriate glue. Fold the excess fabric or paper under, then glue to the inside and bottom of the box.

Cover the top of the lid with fabric or paper, using a light coat of appropriate glue. Clip the excess paper or fabric every inch or so, then fold these tabs over onto the rim, and glue.

Cut paper or fabric to cover the rim of the box lid, taking care to match patterns and conceal raw edges. Fold the top of the paper or fabric under before gluing the strip to the rim.

Glue the raw bottom edges of the paper or fabric to the inside of the lid.

A Blast from the Past

When my husband is away, I sometimes spend the night in the guest bedroom in the old-fashioned double bed I used before I was married. It has a fluffy comforter, ruffled pillow shams, and pretty sheets. If I adjust the mini-blinds just right, I get a lovely view of the treetops and city lights, instead of the tar-and-gravel rooftops and power lines I see during the day. And because there is only one outlet in the room, just enough for a lamp and a clock, I read in bed rather than watch TV. Spending the night in the guest room makes me feel as though I'm staying at a bed and breakfast inn.

No day is so bad that it can't be fixed by a nap.
—CARRIE SNOW

Sleep Potion

Here is a wonderful aromatherapy spray, from *Seasons of Aromatherapy* by Judith Fitzsimmons and Paula Bousquet, that will relax you and help you drift off.

    2 drops chamomile essential oil
    4 drops lavender essential oil
    3 drops orange essential oil
    5 ounces water

Mix all ingredients in a spray bottle. Spray bed clothing and room air before bedtime.

The Delights of Scent

From time immemorial, scent has been used as an aphrodisiac. Time-tested fragrances include amber, ambergris, jasmine, lily of the valley, musk, myrrh, orange blossom, patchouli, sandalwood, and tuberose. Contemporary "erotically oriented" perfumes include Eau Sauvage, Magic Noire, and Poison, each of which contain some of these ancient aphrodisiacs. Besides perfume, try essential oils in a diffuser in the bedroom or burning incense.

> *Eros, the god of love, emerged to create the earth.*
> *Before, all was silent, bare, and motionless.*
> *Now, all was life, joy, and motion.*
> —EARLY GREEK MYTH

The Language of Love

Words do make the mood. We all know the usual terms of endearment—honey, dear, sweetie, angel. But to fan the flames of ardor and romance, why not try some less tired language, like *sweeting, sweetling,* or *sweetkin* (in vogue in the sixteenth and seventeenth centuries). Or how about *dearling* (the original form of *darling*)? Your partner could become your *paramour* (literally "through love" in French).

Instead of attractive or cute, you could try *toothsome* or *cuddlesome*. Rather than *missing*, try *yearning, pining, longing*, or *hungering*, and watch the passion build.

Candles for Romance

Every year for my birthday, my husband buys me a beautiful candle. One year it was a gold angel. Another year it was a heavenly Casablanca lily-scented white one that is still my all-time favorite. This year it was a delicate Japanese paper shade that slips over a votive candle. I put them on the mantel above our bed, and before we make love, he very carefully lights them all. The flickering light, the delicious aroma—what could be more romantic?

Homemade Delight

Surprise your sweetheart with a candlelit dinner for two with your own homemade scented candles gracing both the table and the bedroom. The candles are incredibly easy to make—you just need to plan in advance. The fragrance will be released as they burn. (If you haven't planned ahead, you can still get some of the effect by sprinkling a drop or two of your favorite essential oil in the melted wax of a plain candle as it burns.) Consider what color you want for your candles—red for passion, perhaps? Z. Budapest, in *Goddess in the Bedroom*, recommends peach because "peach has a stabilizing effect that helps to provide a calm atmosphere. It resonates comfort, safety, and well-being. Peach will reassure your lover that you are trustworthy and that you only have eyes for him or her."

Scented Candles

> 2 ounces of your favorite fragrance essential oil (or try a combination—vanilla and rose are my personal favorites for romance)
>
> ¼ cup orrisroot powder (available at herbal stores)
>
> 1 large airtight plastic container big enough to fit the candles you choose
>
> 6 unscented candles, any size

Combine the oil(s) and the orrisroot, and sprinkle in the bottom of the plastic container. Place candles inside the container, cover, and store in a cool spot for 4–6 weeks.

> *How beautiful it is to do nothing,*
> *and then rest afterward.*
> —SPANISH PROVERB

The Nesting Instinct

I love to think of my bed as a nest. With birds as inspired teachers, I carefully choose my sheets, pillows, and covers—cotton and down are my twigs and straw. I don't just make my bed anymore—I build it. That tired task of tidying up the bed is now a flurry of fluffing, tucking, and smoothing that holds a certain charm for me.

I also view the experience of getting into my bed as anything but common. Bedtime is a luxury—a retreat for sweet dreams, warm embraces, and cozy relaxation. There is nothing like curling up in my nest with my husband at the end of the day. Part of our bedtime almost always includes a conversation about how good our bed feels, how cozy we are, and how blessed we are to be in bed together. This exchange has become a little ritual that we indulge in before we go to sleep. The best part of this newfound source of pleasure is that we didn't buy anything or change anything—we simple changed our minds.

A Basket of Love

Want to surprise your paramour some evening? Make a love basket.

Simply find a heart-shaped basket, spray-paint it red (sandpaper it slightly first so the paint will stick better), add a pretty ribbon to the handle, and fill it with your beloved's favorite things: chocolate-covered cherries, sexy underwear, whatever he or she fancies. Then put it on the pillow to be discovered.

Personalized Furniture

We don't have a lot of money. So when I was pregnant, my husband and I hit all the garage sales looking for nursery items. We found an old chest of drawers for $20 and painted it white. When the baby was born, we dipped her hands and feet in water-based, latex pastel paints and then gently stamped her hand- and footprints on the top and sides of the dresser. Now we have a permanent reminder of her babyhood that she, and we, will treasure always.

> *To be simple is to be great.*
> —RALPH WALDO EMERSON

The Pleasures of a Good Book

I read out loud to my sixteen-year-old son every night before he goes to sleep. We read whatever his American Classics teacher has demanded of him. For that half-hour, there's only Steinbeck's words, the lyrical flow of F. Scott Fitzgerald, or the amazing mind of J. D. Salinger.

Eye Pads

These are great for those of us who use our eyes a lot—and who doesn't? Lie down for fifteen minutes with these covering your eyes and presto—you'll feel rejuvenated.

2 10-by-10-inch pieces of muslin

4 ounces dried chamomile flowers

With a pencil and ruler, on both pieces of fabric, mark off 2-inch squares with ⅜-inch seam allowances around each square. You should have 32 squares. Place one of the pieces of muslin down and put 1 teaspoon chamomile in the center of each marked square. Cover with the other piece of muslin and pin. Sew along the guidelines you have made for yourself. Cut apart. Makes 16.

To use, place 2 eye pads in a small bowl and pour 1 tablespoon of boiling water over pads. Cover and let sit until lukewarm. Squeeze gently and apply to closed eyelids for 15 minutes.

The Beauty of Bed

When I was a senior in college I hurt my back. It was the first time my body ever betrayed me. Until then, I always considered it just a handy container to take my mind where it wanted to go. And boy, was that mind busy—valedictorian of my high school class, in the top ten percent of my Ivy League college. But suddenly I couldn't move. At all.

First I spent a week or so flat on my back. Then I'd be up for a few days and then down again. Every time I went to see a doctor (and there were many), they'd tell me to lie down if it hurt. Eventually I spent about a year in bed. Fortunately I then went to a pain clinic and learned how to manage the pain and have a life. But that enforced time on my back made a convert out of me—I realized that I love lying in bed (well, as long as it is voluntary). There is something about being supported by the bed, with no need to hold myself up, that sends delicious shivers up and down my whole body. It's the only time I really let go completely, sinking into the slightly soft yet still-firm mattress. I can spend a day like that!

Sleep Pillows

Sleep pillows go back to Colonial times. They were herb-filled pillows that were used by the ill to help them sleep. But you don't have to be sick to enjoy the benefits! Just put one under your regular pillow so that each time you move your head the luscious scent is released. Here are two recipes you might try.

Lemony Dreams

1 cup dried peppermint

1 cup dried lavender

1 cup lemon verbena or lemon balm

1 cup dried lemon or orange peel, ground

1 10-by-8-inch piece of muslin

Combine all herbs in a bowl and stir with a wooden spoon. Make sure there are no sharp twigs. Fold the muslin in half and sew up two sides. Add the potpourri and slip stitch the open end. The pillow should be relatively flat. Makes 1 pillow.

Hops Help

Hops is said to be mildly sleep-inducing, while lavender induces a sense of well-being. Together they make a great sleep pillow.

1 10-by-8-inch piece of muslin

4 handfuls dried hop flowers

2 handfuls dried lavender

Fold the muslin in half and sew up two sides. Add the hops and lavender and slip stitch the open end. The pillow should be relatively flat. Makes 1 pillow.

Line Them Up

About once a year, I love to organize my sock drawer and throw out the socks that have not had a match for months. It gives me such a sense of satisfaction.

A Feast of Words

Between work and my two kids, my idea of a good time these days is to stay in bed as long as possible in the morning, reading a good book. I can never get enough of it. Sometimes I even wake up in the middle of the night and read for a couple hours just to get my fix. For my birthday, my husband entertained the kids so I could stay in bed with a thick thriller all day. What fun!

> *You can't get spoiled if you do your own ironing.*
> —MERYL STREEP

Laundry Love

I always sort the laundry on my bed. I dump the pile of clean clothes on the bed and put my nose in the warm, dry pile.

Spiced Sachets

These are great for underwear drawers for men and women, but they will also work in closets or suitcases.

6 whole nutmegs

5 cinnamon sticks

1 tablespoon anise seed

1 tablespoon whole allspice

4 vanilla beans, cut in small pieces

½ cup whole cloves

½ cup orrisroot

fabric scraps

ribbons

One after another, place nutmegs, cinnamon sticks, anise, and allspice in double plastic bags; pound with a hammer on a cutting board, then place in large bowl. Add cloves and vanilla beans, mix well with a wooden spoon, then stir in orrisroot. Store in covered jars and shake once a day for 1 week, then once a week for 5 weeks.

When potpourri is ready, create the sweet bag. Cut fabric into two 4-by-8-inch rectangles. On each piece, fold down one of the 4-inch sides 2 inches, right side out, and stitch—this fold is the top of the sachet. Place the pieces of fabric together, right side in, and stitch together the bottom and sides.

Turn right side out, fill half-full, and tie with ribbon.

Custom Quilt

I love making something plain beautiful. Recently I had great success making a one-of-a-kind comforter. I bought an inexpensive, plain blue comforter, a bit of silver fabric, white fabric paint, and glow-in-the-dark fabric paint. I painted on stars with the white paint, interspersing a few glow-in-the-dark stars, and sewed on a moon made out of the silver fabric. The comforter turned out so well that everyone who sees it begs me to make one for them.

In the Mood

Sometimes nighttime can be particularly still and profound. When I feel quiet inside and want to prolong that silence a little before going to sleep, I like to light candles in my bedroom, get into bed, and listen to choral music. I make sure that I can turn off the music and blow out the candles from where I am; the trick is not to have to get up again. I do understand what the composer of "Silent Night" was aiming for, even if he didn't quite pull it off. Other times, night can have a kind of wild, uncontrolled energy which calls for LOUD jazz, R&B, rock— or whatever feeds the excitement—or else scaring myself to death with ghost stories.

Meaningful Wallpaper

I read a wonderful idea in *365 Days of Creative Play* by Sheila Ellison and Judith Gray that I decided to do with my kids. All you do is ask your child to draw pictures of the meaningful things in his or her life, like hopes and dreams, beliefs, loved ones. Then make a border at the top of your child's room with the pictures. I've started doing that with my son. He works on it every few days or so and right now we are about halfway around a wall. It's a great way for a kid to decorate his or her own bedroom.

Flower Tiebacks

I love the romantic look of lace curtains in my bedroom. Recently I came across a wonderful rose tieback that is so easy to make and looks great against the lacy fabric. It's delicate, so once they are on the curtains, you won't want to be taking them on and off all the time.

½-inch wide satin ribbon

moss

small dried roses

Tie a length of ribbon around the curtain you want to tie back and cut to correct length. Mark the area that covers the front of the curtain with two straight pins, one on either end.

Glue small pieces of moss to the area between the two pins. Glue roses attractively into the moss. Trim any moss that is unsightly with scissors. Tie onto curtain. Makes 1 tieback.

Airing Out

I love to open all the windows and doors to get the freshness of the outside air into my bedroom—especially in spring.

> *Mutual pleasures are the sacred core of life: food,*
> *body warmth, love, and sex. . . . These things are*
> *sacred because they are necessary, because they*
> *confer pleasure in the giving and the receiving,*
> *so it is impossible to say who is giving*
> *and who is receiving.*
> —MARILYN FRENCH

Late Night Love Notes

Last Valentine's Day I started a new tradition with my husband. I gave him a little journal that was to be used only for writing love notes to one another. We keep it in the bedside table drawer, and whenever we feel compelled, we make an entry then hide it under the other person's pillow. There's nothing like getting into bed and feeling that little lump under your head and realizing that you have sweet words from your beloved to read before going to sleep.

Custom Curtains

My daughter wanted new curtains, so I took an old bed sheet and cut it to size for the window. After dying it a pastel green, we used sponges of teddy bears, ducks, bunnies, cats, and horses dipped in acrylic paints to create a design that she just loved. It only took one afternoon.

> *To affect the quality of the day;*
> *that is the art of life.*
> —HENRY DAVID THOREAU

Consider Color

Color therapy is the practice of using color for emotional, physical, and spiritual well-being. Each color affects us differently, as do various shades and tones. Some get us excited, others calm us down. The conscious use of color in decor in public places is well documented—fast food joints, for example, are renown for using a vibrant red/orange palette to help us eat fast and move on. Studies in prisons have shown that inmates are more violent in bright red rooms and less in light pink rooms. Those of us who want to get maximum pleasure from our homes should take the emotional effect of color schemes into account, particularly in the bedroom, where we spend so much of our time. In choosing a scheme, remember: Warm colors make people feel productive and energetic; cool colors are soothing and relaxing; dark colors can be depressing; and clear colors are the most uplifting.

Red: People who are anxious or fearful should not use red since it can enhance those feelings. It should not be overly used in rooms other than exercise rooms, but it can be good in a dining room, since it increases appetite and thirst. It has aphrodisiac qualities, so it can also be used in moderation in bedrooms.

Blue: The color of introspection, blue is good for bedrooms of people who have trouble falling asleep; it is sedating and restful. Blue is not good for people suffering from depression; it will enervate them more.

Yellow: Dimly lit rooms would do well being painted yellow. It is also a good color for rooms where mental acuity is important—a home office, for example. Yellow is good for people who take life too seriously and need to have more fun.

Green: The color of healing, green rooms give a sense of health and cleanliness. It's good in rooms where people congregate, such as family rooms and living rooms, since it promotes cooperation.

Orange: Orange represents a blend of the vibrancy of red with the intellect of yellow. Good in the kitchen and where people socialize, orange represents happiness, health, and enthusiasm. It's good for relieving depression and fostering optimism.

Purple: Considered a "feminine" color, purple is said to increase creativity, foster spirituality, and overcome lethargy. It's good for rooms where creative work is done but should be avoided by those prone to depression.

> *Wild nights should be our luxury!*
> —EMILY DICKINSON

Setting the Scene

If you want great sex, it's a good idea to give some thought to creating a bedroom that's conducive to intimacy, says Will Ross in *The Wonderful Little Sex Book*. "It doesn't need to be elaborately furnished, but it should be uncluttered, have pleasing colors, and not be merely utilitarian; it should inspire a sense of beauty. The bed you use for sex ought to have a special, exotic, other-worldly feeling, almost evocative of an altar. There should be an air of reverence. Some people enjoy making love under a canopy, and you may want to construct one. Soft lighting is immensely helpful, and so is quietly pulsating music. When the whole room feels like a retreat from the hustle and bustle of everyday life, won't you relish the thought of spending time there with your beloved?"

Good Books

In their book *The Art of Conscious Loving,* Tantric teachers Caroline and Charles Muir make the following suggestions for a more meaningful connection: Be love- and nurture-oriented rather than goal-oriented, be sure to give and receive, and remember to make love a dance. Other good books on sexual intimacy are *Soulful Sex* by Dr. Victoria Lee, *The Art of Sexual Ecstasy* and *The Art of Sexual Magic* by Margo Anand, and *Sexual Secrets* by Nik Douglas and Penny Slinger.

Door Bouquets

Door bouquets are informal arrangements of dried flowers and grasses tied with raffia or twine and are a wonderful way to bring the beauty of your garden into the house. (If you don't grow flowers, you can buy them already dried and proceed from there.) They are meant to be hung over the top of a mirror or bedpost or hung from a door or doorknob, either outside or inside. The trick is to bunch the flowers together with the longest stems on the bottom and the shortest stems on the top so all the flowers can be seen. In her book *The Scented Room,* Barbara Milos Ohrbach suggests the following bouquet that deters moths and insects from the bedroom closet. No matter what flowers you choose, you can follow the directions below for construction.

Closet Door Bouquet

Take 1 full, long-stemmed sprig each of tansy, wormwood, southernwood, lavender, Silver King artemisia, and rosemary. Air dry by hanging upside down for up to a few weeks. Arrange the dried sprigs in a bunch with the shortest stems on top. Fasten them tightly with a rubber band. Knot a length of twine over the rubber band and wind around the stems for about 1½ inches to hide the rubber band. Knot the twine a second time and make a bow or loop.

Glowing Dreams

Growing up, I had those glow-in-the-dark stars pasted up on my bedroom ceiling. I swear they gave my mother at least as much enjoyment as they gave me. She loved to come in my room and look at them. So when I got into high school and learned that there was glow-in-the dark paint, I decided to surprise her. One weekend when she was out, I painted stars, moons, and planets on her ceiling. That night when she went to bed, was she ever pleasantly surprised!

*Years may wrinkle the skin, but to give up
enthusiasm wrinkles the soul.... Whether seventy
or sixteen, there is in every being's heart a love of
wonder; the sweet amazement at the stars and
starlike things and thoughts; the undaunted
challenge of events, the unfailing childlike
appetite for what comes next, and the
joy in the game of life.*
—SAMUEL ULLMAN

THE BATHROOM

The way to health is to take an
aromatic bath and scented
massage every day.

—HIPPOCRATES

The Rewards of Cleaning

Cleaning the bathroom is my least favorite household chore. Sometimes I coax myself into doing it by offering myself a reward at the end. When everything is clean and shining, I turn on the shower until the room is filled with steam, light the three candles that are distributed throughout the room, prepare a set of soft and freshly washed clothes, and then take a long shower that makes use of all my favorite creams, shampoos, and soaps.

Cleaning Solutions

Looking for assistance (the written kind) on cleaning every room in your house? Check out Jeff Campbell's book *Household Solutions That Work* or the Web site **www.the-cleanteam.com**. *Consumer Reports' How to Clean Practically Anything* is also great. If you want only nontoxic solutions, *Clean and Green* by Annie Berthold-Bond has wonderful ideas that really work.

Water is the most healing of all remedies and the
best of all cosmetics.
—ARAB PROVERB

Breathe and Relax

Whenever I'm feeling crabby or overstretched, I like to take a *long* hot bubble bath. I bring a magazine or book, something to drink, and my favorite soothing music tapes. Sometimes I even bring the phone in too, or better yet, ignore it completely. I alternate between reading lazily and lying on my back with my head halfway underwater so my ears are submerged. I listen to the sound of the water, breathe, and relax. When the water gets cold, I add more hot water. An hour can easily drift away.

Lavender Bath Talc

This is a delicious treat after a long soak.

mortar and pestle

$\frac{1}{3}$ cup dried lavender

$1\frac{1}{4}$ cups cornstarch

25 drops lavender essential oil

small box and ribbon

With a mortar and pestle, grind the lavender into a fine dust. Mix together with the cornstarch. Stirring constantly, slowly add the essential oil drops and mix well. Place in a beautiful box and tie with a ribbon.

Homemade Bubble Bath

In eighteenth-century France, bathing was a social pastime. It was customary among the nobility to receive guests while lounging in the bath, a large part of which was covered for decency sake. In the twentieth century, at least in the movies, people perfected the art of bathing in relative modesty in a bath so full of bubbles that no "indecent" body parts could be seen. This bubble bath is something even tiny kids can make. The trick is to have a pretty container to put it in and to never tell how you did it.

> 2 cups Ivory (or other unscented) dishwashing liquid
> ⅛ ounce of your favorite essential oil (vanilla is my favorite)

Drop the oil into dishwashing liquid, cover, and let sit for 1 week. Pour into a beautiful bottle and add a gift tag, ribbon, and instructions to use ¼ cup per bath. Makes 8 baths.

Flushing the Mind

I do my best thinking while cleaning the toilet bowl. When I'm performing this mindless, distasteful task, I escape the monotony by daydreaming, reflecting, and fantasizing. I flush my mind.

One is happy as the results of one's own efforts.
—GEORGE SANDS

A Bit of Green

I love plants and have them in every room in my house. I especially love placing them in the nice sunny window of my bathroom. They love the moisture, and they have a greater chance of being watered regularly since the water source is right there to remind me. I've had to put up a note to guests, however, to resist the temptation to water the African violets in the guest bathroom—they don't like to get too wet, and overzealous plant-unaware visitors have killed quite a few.

Free Spirit

I like to think outside the box when it comes to my home. I don't like to be restricted by conventional uses of rooms and items; rather, I like to think in terms of the space with which I have to work. This past Christmas I hung tree ornaments in my bathroom. I have a wide plank above the sink, and it was the perfect spot for ornament display. I couldn't stand my bedroom closet doors—in a word, they just seemed dowdy. I took them down and replaced them with a beautiful canvas shower curtain with ties because I couldn't find the right "conventional" curtain.

> *A bathroom should be sterile and beautiful*
> *and functional. It should exude*
> *Japanese-style purity.*
> —FASHION DESIGNER ISAAC MIZRAHI

Simply Scentsational

When I was growing up, any time it was a special occasion, my mother would take out her beautifully carved crystal perfume bottle that was stored in a purple velvet box in the second drawer of the bathroom cabinet, and apply a few drops of the best-smelling perfume in the world to her wrists and neck. My sister and I would stand in the bathroom with her, watching her apply her makeup and inhaling the exotic aroma of the elixir in the magic bottle. To this day, Shalimar is the only perfume I really enjoy, and, like my mother, I use it sparingly (a small bottle lasted me over ten years)—that's what makes it special. But I have learned that if I want the scent to remain pure year after year, I need to keep it in the fridge. It requires a quick trip out of the bathroom to apply, but that's a small price to pay.

I've also figured out that one of the "tones" that makes Shalimar so appealing to me is bergamot, a wonderfully floral yet earthy scent used for centuries in a variety of ways. (It's what gives Earl Gray tea, for example, which I also love, its distinctive taste.) Recently I discovered that bergamot is available in an essential oil. That must be why I love the relaxing bath formula below.

A letter is an unannounced visit; the mailman,
the mediator of impolite incursions. One ought to
have one hour every eight days for receiving
letters, and then take a bath.
—FRIEDRICH NIETZSCHE

Calming Bath

The sensual delight of taking a bath in aromatic oils goes back to the Romans who raised bathing to a high art. The public baths had four parts: first you went to the *unctuarium,* where you were anointed in oils. Then you proceeded to the *frigidarium,* where you took a cold bath, then the *tepidarium* for a tepid one, and you finished with a hot bath in the *caldarium.* While we don't bathe as the Romans did, we can indulge in the essence of the practice.

    4 drops bergamot essential oil
    4 drops lavender essential oil
    2 drops clary sage essential oil

Run a warm bath. Drop the essential oils into the stream of water. Slide in and relax for 10–15 minutes.

Skin Soothing Bath

Here's a great one for the winter, when skin gets so dry.

    1 cup buttermilk
    3 tablespoons Epsom salts
    ½ tablespoon canola oil
    soothing essential oil of your choice, such as lavender or chamomile

Combine ingredients together and pour into the stream of warm water as the tub is filling. Immerse and relax for 10–15 minutes.

The Pleasures of Pampering

I'm a very straightforward woman when it comes to beauty. I don't wear makeup, don't own a blow dryer, and in general, spend a maximum of ten minutes in the bathroom each morning—and that's *with* taking a shower. Maybe that's why, when I'm feeling low, particularly on a dark winter's day, I like to lock myself in the bathroom and pretend I'm at a beauty spa and am having the *full* treatment. I pluck my eyebrows, give myself a facial complete with a mask and a steam cleaning, deep condition my hair, shower using a loofah and heavenly scented body polish, and take a pumice stone to my heels and ankles. I finish off with my favorite body lotion and face cream, feeling pampered and beautiful from head to toe.

On our skin, as on a screen, the gamut of life's experiences is projected: emotions surge, sorrows penetrate, and beauty finds its depth.
—A. MONTAGU

Facial Sauna

 2 drops fennel essential oil
 2 drops lavender essential oil
 2 drops lemon essential oil
 2 drops orange essential oil

Mix oils together and pour into a bowl of steaming water. Drape a towel over your head and the bowl and sit, allowing the steam to penetrate your pores. Be careful not to put your face too close—this should be a luxurious feeling, not a painful one!

Oatmeal Masks

Masks are used to deep-clean and condition the face and should always be applied after you have thoroughly washed. Be sure to avoid your eyes. After applying the mask, lie down for fifteen minutes with your eyes covered with water-moistened eye pads. What kind of mask you choose depends on your skin type. This one works for all types—and it's so easy to make.

$\frac{1}{2}$ cup water

$\frac{1}{4}$ cup oatmeal

Bring water to a boil, add oats, and cook over medium heat about 5 minutes, stirring occasionally. Allow to cool until warm but not hot. Apply to clean skin and leave on 15 minutes. Rinse with warm water, then cool water.

Sensual Bath

2 drops cedar essential oil

2 drops clary sage essential oil

2 drops lavender essential oil

2 drops orange essential oil

2 tablespoons vegetable oil

Combine all oils and pour into the stream of a warm bath.

Hair Moisturizer

Rosemary is very good for hair, particularly dark hair to which it imparts a wonderful shine. It will also help cut down on the problem of flyaway hair. This makes enough for several applications:

8 drops cedar essential oil

8 drops lavender essential oil

12 drops rosemary essential oil

2 tablespoons olive oil

In a small glass container, mix the essential oils together. Add olive oil. Pour about a teaspoon into the palm of your hand and rub hands together. Massage your head, hair, and scalp with the blend. Put a shower cap or warm towel on your head and leave it for 15 minutes. Wash and rinse your hair twice.

Floral Splash

It's easy to make your own eau de cologne, what with all the available essential oils. Here's one version, but feel free to experiment with the essential oils of your choice. If you find this too strong, just dilute with bottled water. A beautiful antique bottle would make the perfect receptacle.

½ cup 100-proof vodka

sterilized wide-neck glass jar with top

20 drops orange essential oil

10 drops bergamot essential oil

10 drops lemon essential oil

2 drops neroli essential oil

¼ cup bottled water without carbonation

paper coffee filter

sterilized decorative glass bottle with top that can hold ¾ cup

Put vodka in a wide-necked jar and add the essential oils, stirring with a wooden spoon. Put lid on and let stand for 2 days. Add water and stir. Cover again and let sit for 4–6 weeks. Strain through a coffee filter and pour into a decorative bottle.

From the Sea

I love to collect shells and sea glass as mementos of my vacations. Being a great beach lover, I have starfish from California, cone shells from Florida and Mexico, a small spineless urchin from Jamaica, and dried sponges from the Adriatic and Mediterranean. I display them on a large shelf above the bathtub. Now when I lie in the tub, I look at my shells and think of all the places I have been, the people I was with, and the good times we had. An advantage that I didn't foresee is that whenever I use the shower, the shells and glass get wet, becoming again the shiny jewels that first caught my eye.

There is no need to go to India or anywhere
else to find peace. You will find that deep place
of silence right in your room, your garden,
or even your bathtub.
—ELISABETH KÜBLER-ROSS

Pine Bath Oil

This is a great skin softener. Just pour a bit into your bath under the running water.

1 cluster pine needles

1 cup baby oil, approximately

Put pine needles in a glass container with a lid. Cover completely with baby oil, and cover the container tightly. Store in dry, cool place for 4 weeks. Strain the oil and decant into an attractive glass bottle. You can add fresh pine needles for decoration. Makes 1 cup.

By Candlelight

I love to bathe solely by candlelight. The warm glow gives a relaxing atmosphere to dream and let stress melt away. I used to live in an apartment with a nice-sized bathroom shelf that accommodated a dozen votives, but recently I moved and there seemed to be no suitable place for my candles. I thought I would have to give up this pleasure, but then I put up corner bracket shelves and mounted candle lanterns on them. Now, even when the candles are not lit, my bathroom has a wonderful exotic flair that everyone comments on!

The human body is the best picture
of the human soul.
—LUDWIG WITTGENSTEIN

Elder Flower Skin Refresher

Here's an old-fashioned skin tonic that is a great gift when packaged in a beautiful glass bottle decorated with an old botanical illustration of an elder flower. Be sure to include storage instructions.

50 elder flower heads, washed in cold water

1 quart jar, sterilized

2½ cups water

5 tablespoons vodka

cheesecloth

decorative glass bottles with lids

Remove the petals from elder flower heads, making sure not to bruise them. Place only the petals in a quart jar. Boil water and pour over the petals. Let stand for 30 minutes and add vodka. Cover and let stand for 24 hours.

Pour the liquid through cheesecloth and into glass bottles. Cap and store in the refrigerator until ready to use. Then keep in a cool, dry, dark place like a cabinet and use within 1 month. Makes 3 cups.

Joy is what happens to us when we allow
ourselves to recognize how good things really are.
—MARIANNE WILLIAMSON

The Art of Aromatherapy

Aromatherapy, the use of scents from the essential oils of plants to alter mood and promote healing, is an ancient art currently enjoying a booming revival. Essential oils are concentrated flower fragrances (1,000 pounds of jasmine flowers makes 1 pound of oil, for example) that are available from catalogs or stores. Good sources include Bare Escentuals (800-227-3990), The Body Shop by Mail (800-541-2535), Casswell-Massey Catalog (800-326-0500), Crabtree & Evelyn Catalog (800-272-2873), Frontier Cooperative Herbs (800-786-1388), Green Mountain Herbs, Ltd. (800-525-2696), Hausmann's Pharmacy, Inc. (800-235-5522), and SelfCare Catalog (800-345-3371).

Most commonly, the oils are used in the bath (put in at the very end and the water should be no more than 100° F), in a diffuser, or placed on a handkerchief and inhaled when you need a lift. Since essential oils are very potent, they should always be diluted with a base oil such as sweet almond or grape seed before being put on your skin. And don't ingest the oil or get it in your eyes. If you are pregnant or have a chronic illness of any kind, consult your physician before using any.

Here are some of the most common essential oils and their qualities:

Basil: uplifting, clarifies thought processes
Bergamot: uplifting yet calming

Cedar wood: relaxing, stress-reducing

Chamomile: soothing and calming, excellent to use after
an argument

Eucalyptus: invigorating, cleansing, tonic

Fennel: relaxing, warming, calming

Fir needle: refreshing, cleansing

Frankincense: calming, releasing fear

Geranium: balancing mood swings, harmonizing

Juniper: purifying, stimulating

Lavender: calming, soothing, relaxing

Lemongrass: stimulating, cleansing, tonic

Lemon: uplifting, refreshing, mental alertness

Lime: invigorating, refreshing

Mandarin orange: uplifting, refreshing

Marjoram: very relaxing, anxiety-reducing

Myrrh: strengthening, inspiring

Orange: uplifting, refreshing

Patchouli: inspiring, sensuous

Peppermint: stimulating, cleansing, refreshing,
invigorating

Pine: refreshing, cleansing, stimulating

Rose: emotionally soothing

Rosemary: stimulating, cleansing, good for studying, invigorating

Sage: cleansing, purifying

Sandalwood: stress-reducing, sensuous, soothing, helps release fear

Spearmint: refreshing, stimulating

Ylang-ylang: uplifting, sensuous

Aromatherapy for Children

With the popularity of aromatherapy these days, many parents are wondering if essential oils are safe for children. Essential oils can be quite strong, so keep the following guidelines in mind if you're using them around children:

1. Always dilute essential oils before applying to children's sensitive skin. You can use oils such as sweet almond, grape seed, or jojoba for massage or skin care and liquid Castile soap for shower products. But never put essential oils directly on a child's skin.

2. Shake well before using because the oils have a tendency to separate.

3. Keep all essential oils and diffusers out of the reach of children. Little children have been known to drink the oils in diffusers.

If you want to be sure the products you're using are safe for kids, try getting a catalog from Aromatherapy for Kids (800-955-8353) or Star Power Essentials (800-457-0904).

The Comforts of Compresses

Compresses—folded towels immersed in water then applied to your face—are one of the easiest natural ways to clean and condition. Plus they feel great! Extremely hot or cold water is not good for your skin; the water temperature should correspond to the state of your skin: cool water decreases circulation and soothes inflammation; warm water increases circulation and encourages glandular activity. You can use plain water or add an essential oil. Since oil and water don't mix, first combine 2–5 drops of the oil (lavender, rose, and neroli are good for all skin types) with a teaspoon of white vinegar and then add to water.

Skin Condition	Water Temperature
Normal	Warm or cool
Oily	Tepid
Dry	Warm
Combination	Warm
Blemishes	Cool or tepid

Herbal Skin Care

Like essential oils, many dried herbs are also good for the skin.
Here are the best herbs for various purposes and skin types:

Cleansing: arnica, calendula, chamomile, comfrey,
  elder flower, lavender, nettle, peppermint, rosemary,
  yarrow

Nourishing: comfrey, ginkgo biloba, ginseng,
  Saint John's wort

Rejuvenating: arnica, calendula, chamomile, comfrey,
  green tea, ginkgo biloba, ginseng, lavender, rosemary

Relaxing: chamomile, lavender, Saint John's wort

Softening: chamomile, lavender, rose, Saint John's wort

Soothing: arnica, calendula, chamomile, elder flower,
  green tea, lavender, rose, witch hazel

Stimulating: gingko biloba, nettle, peppermint, rosemary

Herbal Cleanser

From the preceding list, decide what kind of herbal mixture you want for your face. Soak 1 heaping teaspoon of an
herb or herb mixture in a cup of whole, unpasteurized milk.
Store in the refrigerator for a couple of hours, then strain and
save milk. To use, rinse your face in warm water and use

cotton balls to apply milk to face, avoiding eyes. Rinse with warm water and then cool water.

Why not seize the pleasure at once?
How often is happiness destroyed by
preparation, foolish preparation!
—JANE AUSTEN

Bubble Fun for Kids

Kids generally love bathtime—well, all but washing their hair. Here are some easy ways to make it even more enjoyable:

- Let your child have a Popsicle while taking a bath. No need to worry about the usual mess.

- Make your own "tub paint." Spray shaving cream into plastic containers and add a drop of food coloring, one color for each container, and blend well. Use only a little food coloring to avoid staining either the kids or the tub. Your kids can then finger paint on the tub, each other, and themselves.

- Here's another version of tub paint. Put a cup of white liquid soap into a variety of plastic containers and add a drop of food coloring to each. Stir. Make sure to clean the tub and the kids well after to avoid staining.

- For colorful bubbles, add just a few drops of food coloring to your child's bubble bath.
- Kids love to blow bubbles, but they can really make a sticky mess. So why not break out the bubble jar while your kids are bathing? No need to worry about cleaning up!

> *Luxury need not have a price—*
> *comfort itself is a luxury.*
> —GEOFFREY BEENE

Easy Refresher

I don't know whether I'm so excited about this because it's fabulous (which I believe it is) or because I invented a beauty product on my own. But last summer, when it was so hot, I got it into my mind (I guess because I read that green tea is good for the skin) to take a spray bottle and fill it with equal parts cooled green tea and water. I sprayed it all over my face—it felt and smelled wonderful. I'm hooked on it now.

THE LIVING AND DINING ROOMS

Their tables were stor'd full,
to glad the sight,
And not so much to feed
on as delight.

—WILLIAM SHAKESPEARE

I Could Have Danced All Night

This is something I do only when I'm alone. I put old Bob Marley tapes on my stereo and dance by myself in the living room. Sometimes, when I'm feeling brave, I even look at myself in the mirror. But mostly I dance with my eyes closed, just feeling the music as it moves through my body.

Made in the Shade

I was looking to spruce up the living room without spending much money. I had a couple of old white lampshades that were getting pretty dirty looking. So I decided to cover them with fabric to give the room a fresh look. They turned out absolutely fabulous—and it was incredibly easy. I am so proud of those shades—every time I look at them I get such a sense of satisfaction that no store- bought lamp could possible give.

The ordinary arts we practice every day at
home are of more importance to the soul than
their simplicity might suggest.
—Thomas Moore

Fabric-Covered Lamp Shade

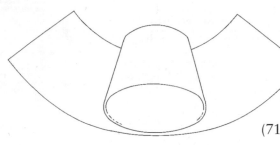

If you would rather make a shade from a kit and are having trouble finding what you want, contact The Lamp Shop in New Hampshire (603-224-1603) or Northland Designs in Wisconsin (715-834-8707).

1 plain, white, unpleated, translucent shade

brown paper

spray glue or fabric glue

about 1 yard lightweight or medium-weight fabric (length depends on size of shade)

First make a pattern by wrapping the brown paper around the shade and taping it in place. Crimp the top and bottom to mark the edges and cut excess.

Remove the paper and trace the pattern on the wrong side of fabric, adding 1 inch to all sides for overlap. Cut out fabric.

Lightly coat the shade with glue. Beginning at the seam line of the shade, press the fabric in place (leaving 1 inch above and below the top and bottom of shade). Carefully wrap the fabric around the shade, smoothing out wrinkles or air bubbles as you go. When you reach the seam line again, fold the end of the fabric under a half-inch and overlap the beginning end, covering it completely. Glue in place. At the top and bottom, clip the fabric every inch or so, then fold down and glue these flaps to the inside.

Balloon Shades

You know those rice-paper balloon shades for ceiling fixtures that are sold at places like Cost Plus and Pier 1 Imports? Well, last year I decided to make some of my own, and boy did they turn out fabulous. It's easy.

flour

glue

water

rice paper or colored tissue paper, cut or torn into strips

1 big balloon, like a punching balloon

Make papier-mâché using a mixture of flour, white glue, and water (twice as much glue and water than flour so the shade will remain translucent); dip the paper in the wet mixture and layer strips of paper onto the balloon. Make sure you leave a big opening where the tie of the balloon is so that you can fit the shade over a light bulb. When the glue is dry and there are enough layers for the shade to be sturdy, deflate the balloon and remove it.

Chocolate-Covered Quiet

I love the silence of the house after everyone has gone to bed. It's my own special private time. I'll unwrap a bar of chocolate (Lindt bittersweet) and curl up on the couch with a chocolate-worthy book, maybe a P. G. Wodehouse or a Dorothy Sayers. And I'll sit there for hours, slowly savoring the chocolate and the stories and relaxing in the silence.

> *Gastronomical perfection can be reached in these combinations: one person dining alone, usually upon a couch or a hillside; two persons, of no matter what sex or age, dining in a good restaurant; six people, of no matter what sex or age, dining in a good home.*
> —M. F. K. FISHER

Pillows of Love

I do needlepoint. I make pillows and pictures for people I care about, my family, and friends. Since I choose a project to suit a particular person, I think about that person and his or her life and our relationship as I work—sometimes for months. I made a memorial pillow for a friend whose teenage daughter died. As I stitched, I thought about her brief life and cried a little for them both. I just finished a cat pillow for a friend who's moving to Chicago and leaving her college-age son for the first time. While I worked on her pillow, I thought about the kind of person she is and what this move means in her life.

Art Pillow

If needlepoint is not your thing, you can make a one-of-a-kind pillow for your living room as easy as pie—all you need is a drawing that you or your child has done and a few items that are available at any fabric store.

1 drawing
1 pillow-sized piece of foam
2 pieces of plain fabric, each 1 inch larger around than the foam
tracing paper
liquid embroidery (available at craft stores)
needle and thread

Find a piece of art that your child has done and likes. Trace it onto one of the pieces of fabric. Using the liquid embroidery, embroider the lines of the drawing onto the fabric. Place the two pieces of fabric together, right side in, and sew on three sides. Turn right side out, insert the foam, and stitch the fourth side.

> *Music acts like a magic key, to which the most tightly closed heart opens.*
> —MARIA VON TRAPP

Our Song

The kids had been packed away to Grandma's, and I was in the kitchen preparing a romantic dinner and asked my husband to put on some music. After what seemed like an unusually long time, I heard the opening bar to an old Beatles song, and with all these powerful emotions swelling up, I turned to see him standing in the living room with a silly grin on his face. It was "our song" from twenty years ago, and we started laughing and crying, remembering the different places we had been and things we had done that were connected to that song.

For the rest of the evening, we traded off picking old songs to play, spilling out memories and sharing old, but suddenly very vibrant, feelings evoked by the magic of the music. We danced some, talked a lot—and never did get around to eating dinner.

Around the Table

I have a staunch rule that I will break only for real emergencies—my family sits down to dinner together at the dining room table every night. If we can't eat together for at least one meal a day, why do we even call ourselves a family? It's our together-time, the four of us around the table—telling jokes we've heard, sharing the news of our day. No TV, phone calls, video games, books—just face-to-face interaction. One of the kids' favorite dinnertime conversations is what I call "Remember When." Someone will start it: "Remember when I was two, Dad, and got the flu and threw up on you?"—the grosser the better for the kids. "Remember when you were trying to hit the golf ball in the living room and broke Mom's best plant?" The half-hour or so we spend together eating, talking, and laughing is what I remember most strongly when I look back over my life. Just the most ordinary together-time.

*I sometimes think that the act of bringing food is
one of the basic roots of all relationships.*
—THE DALAI LAMA

Heart Place Mats

This is a lovely item that will grace your table for months to come.

tracing paper

Scotch tape

2 15-by-19-inch pieces of washable fabric, red or patterned with hearts

thread to match

straight pins

Tape two 8½-by-11-inch pieces of tracing paper together along the 8½-inch sides. Fold in half along the tape seam and cut out a heart. Unfold the paper, trace the heart onto the wrong side of the fabric pieces, and cut out the fabric.

Place the two hearts together, right side in, and pin together. Stitch along the outside of the heart, a quarter-inch from the edge, leaving an opening of about 2 inches. Clip along the curved edges and in the crevice. Turn right side out and slip stitch the opening. Makes 1 place mat.

The Party Fan

Beautifully folded napkins add to the beauty of any place setting. Here's one that takes no time at all. If you don't have napkin rings, use a bit of ribbon or raffia as a tie.

First fold the napkin in half to form a rectangle that is wider than it is tall. Fold the rectangle into 1-inch accordion pleats and hold with a ring or ribbon. Spread out the pleats at the top and bottom to create a fan.

> *If the day and the night are such that you greet*
> *them with joy, and life emits a fragrance like*
> *flowers and sweet-scented herbs,...*
> *that is your success.*
> —HENRY DAVID THOREAU

Basking in the Glow

My favorite time of day is the early afternoon when the sun is low enough to reach into the deepest corner of our living room. The deep colors of the room—browns, reds, and yellows—are enhanced and shine even warmer than usual. I like to stand in the middle of the room and look at the light reflecting on the walls. It is then that I feel strongest that I have made a comfortable nest for myself, and the sense of satisfaction that this gives me stays until the light fades.

Candy-Coated Fun

I have a great big candy bowl that I keep on my living room coffee table. Whoever ends up sitting on my sofa eventually rummages through the bowl for their favorites. I always keep it filled with a varied selection of small, individually wrapped items—bubble gum, fireballs, peppermints, lifesavers, chocolate, and lollipops—and make sure they're all fresh. It's a fun treat.

Va-Va-Va-Voom

I love vacuuming. Vacuuming marks a path and covers the ground. You see the entire pattern—you see where you've been and where you're going. Try sprinkling some deodorant powder about. Utter satisfaction. Or try more advanced vacuuming: creating new patterns, finding the most efficient path, the most serpentine. Try to vacuum the entire room without crossing any previously vacuumed paths. Vacuum the kitchen linoleum. Take a small portable vacuum with a wide attachment and vacuum a placid cat. Remove the attachment and see if the hose will suck onto your forearm (be careful not to leave it on for any length of time unless you want a hickey). Vacuum your car and discover lost treasure.

Unfortunately, my current home has hardwood floors. I'm looking to move.

A dinner invitation, once accepted, is a sacred
obligation. If you die before the dinner takes
place, your executor must attend.
—WARD MCALLISTER

The Delights of Dinner Parties

I love to put on dinner parties—small affairs for four to eight people that allow for meaningful conversation and do not require much work for me. I even bought an old pine table that seats ten, and when I was looking for a new house, a dining room that would accommodate the table was one of my highest priorities. I guess I love dinner parties because I like to cook for an audience—it's fun to try out new dishes and see the pleasure friends get from eating my food. I must confess I always experiment on guests (supposedly a party no-no), trying something fancy that caught my eye, which can be cause for alarm when it doesn't work out the way I planned. But how else will I ever get a chance to try that rib roast recipe I found in *Sunset,* with juniper berries, that is set aflame with gin just before serving? I certainly can't make it just for myself. Fortunately most of my friends are adventurous eaters, willing to take culinary risks.

But there have been some disasters—most recently an overly salty pork loin that I left in the brine too long before barbecuing. But the four of us at that dinner laughed, ate a lot of rice and vegetables, drank red wine, and had a great time just being together. (And I got "credit for trying," as my friend Bill put it.) And that's really what dinner parties are about— enjoying one another's company.

Come, let us dance, and make a feast of joy!
—RUSSIAN TOAST

Tulip Pots

These make a beautiful natural decoration for your dining table, sideboard, or coffee table. It's particularly cheerful in the winter when the prospect of spring seems far off. It does take some advanced planning, but that's part of the fun.

9 tulip bulbs
potting soil

sand

3 8-inch pots

sphagnum moss

Buy the tulip bulbs around Thanksgiving and let them sit in your refrigerator until 6–8 weeks before you wish them to bloom.

Create the potting mix by combining 3 parts potting soil with 1 part sand. As you put this mixture into the pots, put 3 bulbs in each pot, halfway down in the soil. Water the pots and place in an area that is protected from the weather. Keep the soil moist. When the shoots come up, bring the pots into the house and cover the soil with sphagnum moss. Water the plants regularly and don't let the soil dry out.

If you want to treat the bulbs as perennials, keep watering the pots for a month after they stop blooming, then stop watering and let the leaves die. Remove the bulbs from the soil and place in a paper bag. Put the bag into a dark, dry place such as a garage or basement. If you live where it freezes, simply leave the bulbs outside in the garage. If you live in a more temperate zone, in order to bloom again properly the bulbs need to be refrigerated at least 4–6 weeks before planting again. After they've been in the cold, pot the bulbs following the potting instructions given.

Love Cloth

Before my son's first birthday I bought a white linen tablecloth. We have since used it only on his birthdays and have invited guests to each year's birthday party to sign their names (or in the case of toddlers, draw something which I then signed) on his tablecloth with permanent markers. Now, ten years later, we have a colorful tablecloth full of memories to last a lifetime. The kids love writing on it and reading all the messages from past birthdays.

One day with life and heart is more than
enough time to find a world.
—James Russell Lowell

Candle Pots

One of the easiest and most attractive arrangements you can make for a table or sideboard is a series of cream or white pillar candles in terra cotta pots. Just group them attractively and you have a simple yet sophisticated adornment. Make sure you never leave the candles unattended; the moss can catch on fire if the candle burns too far down.

    dry floral foam
    1 terra cotta pot

green, sphagnum, or reindeer moss

1 pillar candle

hot-glue gun

floral pins or straight pins

Trim the foam to approximately the same shape as the pot, making sure it is a little larger than the pot's diameter. Push the foam firmly into the pot until it touches the bottom. Trim if needed to get a good fit. Pack any spaces around the foam with moss. Trim the top of the foam level with the pot. Hot-glue the candle to the foam. Surround the base of the candle with moss, fixing it in place with pins. Makes 1.

Candle Collars

Another wonderful way to dress up pillar candles is to make a candle collar. The candle must be fat enough to be safe and, again, you should never leave it unattended. To avoid accidents, make sure you place the candle on a dish so that the hot wax won't spread all over and snuff out the candle when there is an inch left at the bottom of the collar.

bay leaves, magnolia, or other attractive oval-shaped leaves

hot-glue gun

pillar candle

raffia

Put a little hot glue on the back of each leaf near the base and press firmly to the candle. Trim the bottom of the leaves so that the candle stands evenly.

Tie raffia in a bow around the leaves and the candle. Makes 1 candle.

Flower Frames

You can beautify family photos by matting them with attractively colored mats and then gluing dried flowers on. A great gift!

mat frames
Spanish moss
dried flowers
hot-glue gun

Find mats that fit the photos you want to frame. Arrange the moss and flowers in an attractive manner on the mat and then hot-glue in place.

Little Lights

I was raised Catholic and loved the votive lights in church. I would always light one when I had spare change. So when stores started selling them a few years ago for home use, I just had to have some. I ran out and bought a dozen of the plain ones and placed them on the mantel of my dining room fireplace. On special occasions—birthdays, Christmas—or whenever if I get in the mood, I light them all before eating. I am still amazed at how much pleasure I get just from looking at them all lit up—a warm, content sense that somehow a bit of holiness has descended into my life.

Floating Candles

Candles do add a magical element to any room. I especially love the floating ones as a centerpiece for the dining room table. It solves the problem of having an arrangement that interferes with conversation. Simply float a few candles and some flowers in a bowl and you have an elegant focal point.

> 12 ounces paraffin
> 60 drops of your favorite essential oil
> 12 metal pastry tins or candle molds
> 12 1-inch floating candle wicks (available at craft stores)

In a double boiler, melt the paraffin and then add the essential oil with a wooden spoon. Pour wax into molds slowly to avoid air bubbles. Let set partly and then insert wicks in the center of each. Let candles set fully and then unmold. Makes 1 dozen.

There is nothing worse for mortals than
a wandering life.
—HOMER

Remains of the Day

My current schedule requires me to get up earlier than my wife
and our two-year-old daughter. I may grumble when the alarm
goes off, but I relish that hour of solitude. It's not just sitting at
the table drinking coffee and reading the paper in silence. Nor
is it the beauty of the morning. What I love is seeing the
remains of yesterday's activities and dramas: the stuffed animal
wrapped in a dishtowel "blanket" on the chair where we left it
last night, the last crackling cinders in the fireplace, a little sock
lying under the table. It's sort of an archaeology of the living. I
see the object and it brings a flood of memories.

We lift our tea cup—of course it is of the finest old
India or Chinese porcelain (egg shell preferred)—
to our lips. Rest—Peace Ambrosia! We are at
one with the gods. They of Olympus with nectar
and damp clouds have nothing on us with
our sparkling fire and tea inspiring
and recreating us.
—ALICE FOOTE McDOUGALL

Simplifying Entertaining

I love to have friends over for dinner but I don't have much time. And I'm not the best chef in the world either. But I accidentally hit upon a method for entertaining that solves all my problems. Over the years I have developed a few "guest menus"—for example, a delicious vegetarian stew for my non-meat-eating friends; that meal begins with a warm goat cheese, garlic, and sundried tomato appetizer that everyone loves and can be made in less than ten minutes. I have a Mexican meal, a meat and potatoes meal (lamb kabobs marinated in cinnamon and vinegar), and a fabulous chicken dish (in which pounded chicken breasts are rolled up with goat cheese and sundried tomatoes—yes, I do love those two things). I've collected each "menu" in a notebook with lists of ingredients needed for each meal and a notation of whom I've served it to. When I'm having guests, I just whip out my notebook, see what I haven't served recently, and shop. It's incredibly easy, and my friends think I'm a fabulous chef. In fact, some items have become my signature dishes—people ask to have specific things or beg me to bring them to potlucks. Here are two of my favorite recipes.

Warm Goat Cheese Appetizer

This is adapted from *Cucina Rustica* by Viana La Place and Evan Kleiman. It never fails to get raves—and requests for the recipe. Serve with crackers or baguettes.

2 tablespoons olive oil

6 garlic cloves, peeled and sliced

8 ounces goat cheese

1 teaspoon dried oregano

5 sundried tomatoes in oil, drained and cut into slivers

2 teaspoons capers

pepper to taste

Heat the oil in a small skillet and sauté the garlic until golden brown. Set aside. Cut the goat cheese into ½-inch thick rounds and place in a single layer in a microwave-safe dish just large enough to hold the cheese. Sprinkle on oregano, tomatoes, capers, and reserved garlic. Grind pepper on top. Heat in the microwave for a minute or so until cheese is warm. Serves 6.

Persian Lamb Kabobs

These are fabulous—and relatively low-fat.

1 pound lamb from leg or loin, trimmed of fat and cut into 1-inch cubes

4 tablespoons red wine vinegar

2 cloves garlic, chopped or pressed

1 teaspoon dried oregano

1/4 teaspoon nutmeg

1 teaspoon cinnamon

6 skewers

1 green or red pepper, cut into chunks

1 large onion, cut into chunks

12 cherry tomatoes

Combine lamb with vinegar, garlic, oregano, nutmeg, and cinnamon. Mix well, cover, and marinate in the refrigerator overnight.

Remove lamb from marinade and thread onto skewers, alternating with pepper, onion, and tomatoes. Brush meat with marinade and barbecue until lamb is medium rare, about 10 minutes, turning every few minutes. Serves 6.

Garden Flower Wreath

With this simple wreath you can have the glory of your summer garden all year round in your living room or dining room. You can also use it as a candle ring by putting it down on the dining room table and placing a large pillar candle in the center. Microwaving your own flowers to dry them is relatively easy but does involve a bit of luck. So keep trying. A note of caution: Don't pick the flowers in the morning or after a rainstorm as there will be too much water in the flower.

cut flowers from your garden or from the store, such as daffodils,
  roses, heather, carnations
brown paper bag
grapevine wreath base
dried flowers of your choice to complement your garden flowers
hot-glue gun

Place the cut flowers in the paper bag. Close the bag and place it in the microwave. On half-power, microwave in1½-minute increments until the flowers have dried. (You may want to take notes as each flower at different stages of blooming takes a different amount of time to dry.) On the grapevine base, arrange the flowers in a pleasing arrangement. Hot-glue the stems of the flowers and insert as you wish into the wreath base.

> *We can only receive what we're*
> *big enough to receive.*
> —MATTHEW FOX

Tea for One

On cold winter nights nothing beats curling up in front of the fireplace with a cup of hot tea and a good book. The mug warms my hand, the delicious liquid warms my insides going down. My personal favorite tea is Earl Gray. I love that flowery mysterious flavor—but no milk and sugar for me! I like mine straight. Recently though, I have been drinking herbal teas—beside the fact that they are caffeine-free, they have all kinds of health benefits. I like to make my own. It's easy—as long as you don't combine different herbs. Just stick to one herb at a time (professionals call them *simples*). There's something about making the *simple* and then drinking it later than feels like a bit of a homey ritual to me.

Herbal Tea Infusions

Start with a handful of dried herb of your choice (see chart following). Place it in a glass jar and put a stainless steel knife into the jar (to keep the glass from cracking). Pour boiling water into the jar and stir. Put a lid on (a plate will do) and let sit until completely cool. Strain and store in the refrigerator. To serve hot, bring to a boil on the stove or in the microwave.

Common Herbs for Teas

Blueberry Leaves: A very delicious tea said to be beneficial for blood sugar problems and varicose veins.

Dandelion Root: High in iron, manganese, phosphorous, calcium, magnesium, zinc, and potassium. A diuretic, it is reportedly good for the liver by helping the body remove toxins.

Echinacea Root: Native Americans used it to heal wounds. Modern folks swear by it when a cold or flu is coming on since it is said to be a booster of the immune-system.

Fennel Seeds and Leaves: Good for the intestinal tract. A natural breath freshener.

Gingerroot: Good for digestion, nausea, and morning sickness. Is also said to aid circulation. Tea with this herb is made differently—simply cut off a slice of the fresh root, pour boiling water over it, and let steep for ten minutes. (You probably will want to add some sweetener like sugar or honey.)

Nettle: Reputed to be good for kidneys and an immune system booster. Is high in many minerals and vitamins including iron, thiamine, and riboflavin.

Buying Herbal Tea

Most health food stores carry herbal teas in bags. But if you want to buy herbs in bulk (store in a dry, dark, glass container), you can contact Blessed Herbs (800-489-4372), Companion Plants (614-592-4643), Granum (206-525-0051), or Herbs, Etc. (505-982-1265).

Cranberry Tea

If your tastes don't run to herbal teas, try this wonderfully spicy potion instead. This makes enough for a crowd—try it on a cold winter's evening. I make it unsweetened and allow guests to add their own sugar if they want. You can make it with decaf bags if you want to avoid the kick.

    4 cups water
    4 cups cranberry juice
    4 orange pekoe tea bags
    ³/₄ teaspoon cinnamon
    16 cloves
    1 apple, cored, seeded, and cut into 8 slices

Bring water and juice to a boil over medium heat. Place the tea bags in the mixture, cover, and remove from heat. Let steep 10 minutes. Remove the bags. Add the cinnamon. Place 2 cloves in each apple slice and add to tea. Let steep 5 minutes. Pour into mugs, making sure each cup gets 1 apple slice. Serves 8.

The Perfect Cup of Tea

Fill kettle with fresh cold water and bring to a roiling boil. Scald tea pot with hot water. Place 1 rounded teaspoon of loose tea per cup into an infuser inside the pot (or 1 tea bag per cup). Pour boiling water into teapot. Let steep for 3 minutes. Remove tea infuser and serve.

Firelight will not let you read stories, but it's warm
and you won't see the dust on the floor.
—IRISH PROVERB

Fun with Fire

We have a beautiful fireplace in our living room, and most winter days I keep a fire going all day and evening long. It becomes the centerpiece around which daily life goes on.

I love building a fire. I think of it like the Japanese tea ceremony, a chance to go slow and give complete awareness to what I am doing. I begin with three or four crumpled-up sheets of newspaper. Then in the center of the fireplace I stack small pieces of wood, the kindling, on top and around the newspaper. My fireplace has a rack on which the wood sits, so I then carefully place a large piece of wood in back of the kindling and one in front of the kindling. I don't believe in store-bought fireplace tools. I feel it is very important to use a fire-stick of your own choosing to work the fire. I use a small branch broken by hand to a perfect length for poking and prodding.

Now the fire is ready to light. As the kindling begins to catch, I add midsized pieces of wood, one or two at a time, either by placing them across the two big pieces or just placing them on top of the burning kindling. This is the time that I have to be mindful of what the fire needs to catch the midsized logs and keep them burning. The fire may need more kindling before the new wood is added, it may need more kindling after the first couple of pieces are added, or it may not need any more kindling at all.

The other thing I keep in mind is the need to create an igloo of wood around the center of the fire. This keeps the heat of the fire concentrated, allowing the heat to increase rapidly and keep the bigger pieces of wood burning. Big wood will not burn on its own without a concentrated heat source.

When I have the midsized pieces of wood burning well, they fall into the center, creating more fuel and allowing me to add the big log onto the top to create a nice warm fire. Here again I must be mindful of what the fire needs to keep burning and not create much smoke. I use my fire-stick to push more midsized pieces of wood into the center, create tunnels for air to get to the center, and turn the big log to keep a fresh side facing in until the fire is big enough to keep burning on its own without smoke.

I love to bring a fire to life and spend many lazy hours keeping it going.

Homemade Fire Starters

Here's a great gift for anyone who has a fireplace or wood-stove.

1 block paraffin
double boiler
food dye
pine or cedar essential oil
old wooden spoon
pinecones
old tongs
waxed paper

Melt the paraffin in the top of a double boiler. Add dye of your choice to color the wax and a few drops of pine or cedar essential oil to scent. Stir with an old wooden spoon. Using the tongs, dip the pinecones in the wax to cover, then set the pinecones on waxed paper to harden.

Delights of Dusting

Dusting the sewing table my great-great-grandfather made for my grandmother, the Victorian table my great-grandmother dusted, and the tacky, tacky frame my best friend sent me with a picture of the two of us down at the beach. Dusting the 1950s rooster lamp that I bought on sale at Woolworth's for $2.99 and carried home on the bus. Dusting the furniture my husband made for me.

Lemon Beeswax Polish

For those who love the glow of freshly polished wood furniture, here's a real treat—homemade furniture polish. Nothing beats the smell of lemon and beeswax!

⅔ cup boiling water

1 tablespoon liquid lemon dish detergent

2 ounces beeswax

½ ounce paraffin

1¼ cups turpentine

10 drops lemon essential oil

wide-neck jar with lid

Pour the boiling water into the dish detergent and allow to cool. In a double boiler, heat beeswax, paraffin, and turpentine over very low heat, taking care that mixture doesn't get hot enough to flare up. Whisk soap water into wax to form an emulsion. Add essential oil. Store in a wide-neck jar with a lid. Makes about 2 cups.

*The smell rejoiceth the heart of man, for which
cause they used to strew [herbs and flowers]
in chambers and places of recreation, pleasure,
and repose, where feasts and
banquets are made.*

—JOHN GERARD

A Bunch of Beauty

Once a week or so I buy flowers at the grocery store and take great pleasure in arranging that fresh bunch of flowers in a vase or two.

The other day at the store, one bunch of particularly vibrant dark pinks was much thicker than usual. I just had to buy it—pinching pennies can be so satisfying! Later I spent twenty minutes at my house happily making one arrangement after another, filling vase after vase. The florist had counted a few too many blooms into the rubber-banded bunch and had given me a bargain both satisfying and beautiful.

Flower Arranging Tips

- Invest in a large beautiful vase—there's nothing like a heavy, well-designed, large, beautiful vase to display flowers and accent a room.

- Make an arrangement with "found" plants. This past Christmas my mother and I took a walk around our street. Someone had been trimming their evergreens and we ended up picking up several branches of different pines that were just lying in the snow. We took them home, she arranged them in a vase with a red bow and a few white mums, and we had an arrangement worthy of Martha Stewart.

- Think all one color of different kinds of flowers—all white flowers, or all red, or all pink. The variety of flowers and the monotone color really work together.

- Use odd numbers to create a pleasing arrangement.

- The highest flower or green should be 2½ times the height of the container, and the largest flowers should be at the bottom of an arrangement.

> *I'd rather have roses on my table than diamonds on my neck.*
> —EMMA GOLDMAN

Homemade Love

We have several pieces of art (paintings, handmade bowls, dry flower arrangements) that were made by friends. Sometimes I just take the "house tour" and look at them and think of the people who made them. This brings back memories of my friends that are more vivid than if I were looking at pictures of them.

Memory Plates

A craft from Victorian times that seems to have gone out of favor is the making of memory plates. These are collages that are made from photos and other paper memorabilia and then attached to the back of a clear glass plate and displayed in the living room or study. They can be very beautiful, because the colors in whatever artwork you've chosen are seen through the glass, making it look as if the artwork is under water.

1 translucent glass plate
photos and images of your choice cut from magazines or catalogs
decoupage fixative (available at craft stores)
tissue paper
spray glue
polyurethane

Create the design you want on a similar-sized plate and then transfer the images one at a time to the glass plate. Apply the decoupage glue to the front of the image and then press the image onto the back of the plate, carefully pressing out any bubbles or wrinkles. When your design is complete, cut out a piece of tissue paper the same size as the plate and glue it to the back of the images, so that from behind you will see only a white surface. Seal the back and the rim of the plate with 3 coats of polyurethane, allowing it to dry completely between coats.

> *Go, eat your food with gladness, and drink your*
> *wine with a joyful heart.*
> —ECCLESIASTES 9:7

Wine Memories

I have a small collection of wines, and sometimes I'll just go over the list or go down to the basement and look at them. They remind me of trips to wineries on hot summer days, wine tasting with friends, and special dinners with my wife. I notice wines I'm saving for people I'm going to see and wines I've shared with people in the past.

A Special Bottle

A friend of mine bought a good bottle of red wine when his son was born, with the intention of opening it with his son on the boy's twenty-first birthday. He kept the bottle in the basement so it would stay cool. His plan inspired me, so I started getting bottles on special occasions to open years later. My husband and I just opened a bottle we'd saved from our wedding to have on our fifth anniversary, and we still have one more for our tenth. Great fun.

All-Purpose Room Spray

When the house feels musty and stale, try this aromatherapy spray to freshen things up a bit. The authors of *Seasons of Aromatherapy* also recommend adding a few drops to your laundry to freshen up the clean clothes.

4 drops lavender essential oil

2 drops peppermint essential oil

2 drops tea tree essential oil

2 cups water

Combine all ingredients in a spray bottle.

Exotic Potpourri

If you like to give your living room an exotic scent, the following potpourri is a wonderful way to do just that. This makes a lot, but it is very long-lasting and makes a great gift.

1 cup orrisroot

2 teaspoons rose oil

4 cups dried rose petals

4 cups vetiver root or vetiver

3 cups patchouli leaves

1 cup sandalwood

2 cups mace

Using a wooden spoon, combine the orrisroot and rose oil in a large, nonmetallic bowl. Add the remaining ingredients and pack into boxes or jars. Let set for four weeks, shaking occasionally. Makes 14 cups.

Potpourri Supplies

If you are having trouble finding the ingredients to make all the wonderful potpourri recipes in this book, write to Lavender Lane, P.O. Box 7265, Citrus Heights, CA 95621 ($2 for catalog); Rosemary House, 120 South Market Street, Mechanicsburg, PA 17055 ($2 for catalog); or Indiana Botanic Gardens, P.O. Box 5, Hammond, IN 46325 (free catalog).

Home Alone

Being home alone and remaining sensitive to the combined energies of one's self, the day, and the house can be an experience of acute living, especially if the environment itself is giving you a strong message or feeling. I often feel madly happy at twilight during the late summer and fall for no other reason than just because I do.

Playing House

When I'm bored, I like to rearrange the furniture in the living room. It just gives me a little lift to see a different configuration and experience the room from a different perspective. I feel more awake, alive.

THE FAMILY ROOM

'Mid pleasures and palaces though
we may roam,
Be it ever so humble, there's no place like home.

—JOHN HOWARD PAYNE

Family Home Evening

I was tired of running all over with all the kids every day—soccer practice, games, piano lessons, tennis, play dates with friends ... the list went on and on. I was exhausted and the kids seemed cranky; there was never any downtime. It seemed as though we never had even one evening to spend together as a family. Then I read about the tradition that Mormons have of a weekly "family home evening" and decided that was just what our family needed. And so I decreed Wednesdays as our "family home evening." After dinner all of us spend the evening together with the TV off, no outsiders, meetings, classes, or other commitments. Sometimes we play cards or a board game, read a story aloud, or tell ghost stories; other times we bake cookies together or just read in the same room. The kids protested at first, but now they too have gotten into the spirit.

There is no such thing as a crash
course in serenity.
—SHIRLEY MACLAINE

Decorative Light Switches

One great activity that families can do together is decorate the light switches in various rooms of the house. All you need is acrylic paints and small brushes. Take the switch off the wall, paint the design of your choice (mistakes wipe off easily with water), let dry thoroughly, and rescrew into the wall.

Rainy Day Treasure Hunt

Sometimes on a rainy day when my kids are bored out of their minds and I want to lure them away from the TV and computer games, I declare it's time for a treasure hunt. They absolutely love it and it's easy to organize (as long as you do it in advance of your announcement, when they are busy in other rooms). All you need is different-colored ribbons—two small pieces of one color for each person. Hide one piece of each color in various locations in designated rooms. Depending on the age of the kids, you can make this relatively easy or incredibly hard. Ribbons can be hidden almost anywhere—in doorjambs, inside lampshades, inside books. You decide whether a piece must be showing or not, again depending on the age and frustration level of the kids. When you've hidden all the ribbons, call the kids and give them a piece of their particular colored ribbon and tell them they have to find the matching piece. When they do, they get a prize. (That way everyone gets a prize.) Alternately, you can hide many pieces of various colors and tell them that they must find one piece of each color; the first person to do so gets a prize.

> *Begin now doing what you want to do now.*
> *We are not living in eternity. We have only this*
> *moment, sparkling like a star in our hand—*
> *and melting like a snowflake.*
> —MARIE BEYNON RAY

The Family Calendar

Between my husband and I and our five kids, our schedule is pretty hectic. So I've learned to sit everyone down once a month and construct a family calendar. We take a big piece of butcher paper and I draw in the days of the month. Then we fill in our various commitments using a sticker to symbolize each of us—I am a red star, my husband blue, the family as a whole is white. The older kids who can write help fill in the details while the little ones place the right colored stars in the boxes. As the month progresses, we just add to the calendar. It's a great way to keep track of everything—and has the added benefit that the making of the calendar is in itself a way for all of us to be together.

Saturday Night at the Movies

We don't have much money, so we are always looking for inexpensive ways to be together. The best one we've come up with so far is "Saturday Night at the Movies." The whole family goes to the video store Saturday afternoon to rent a video that we might all like (this can take awhile). Then we come home and have dinner on trays in the family room as we watch the video together. Popcorn as dessert is a must. It's amazing how eating in front of the TV (which we do not allow the rest of the week) is such a treat for the kids!

Simplicity is the essence of happiness.
—CEDRIC BLEDSOE

Dress Up—or Down

One of the great joys of my childhood was playing dress-up with my sister. We would clomp around in our mother's old high heels and negligees, with purses on our arms, feeling oh so elegant. Our favorite thing was to get dressed ourselves, then dress our long-suffering orange tabby in old baby clothes and put her in the baby carriage or doll cradle and play Mom. (The cat apparently wasn't too tortured—he actually took up sleeping in the cradle on his own.) I can still recall the toybox in the family room that we kept the clothes in—a faded, plastic-covered trunk with pink and white flowers. Now that I have a daughter of my own, I've started saving some old "treasures" for when she gets a bit older—hats, scarves, purses, nightgowns, dresses, jewelry, shoes. I hope she'll enjoy dress-up as much as I did.

Time Capsule

We recently did a family time capsule and all three kids—ages five, seven, and twelve—really enjoyed it. I took an old trunk and had each child and my husband and I put in something to represent ourselves right now—something we considered important. We then put in the day's newspaper, a grocery store receipt (my twelve-year-old's idea to compare prices now and then), and photos of ourselves we recently took. Then we sealed it and put a note saying we would open it in 2015, sixteen years from now. We all had a great time together deciding what we wanted to include.

*How nice it is, in a world filled with mean,
scary people like landlords, motor vehicle bureau
personnel, and headwaiters, to set aside
time for milk and cookies.*
—JANE AND MICHAEL STERN

The Comfy Couch

What greater pleasure does life have to offer than a midafternoon Saturday nap on a comfy couch? The delicious feeling of knowing that you should be up doing chores but instead are stretched out supine, luxuriating in doing absolutely nothing. Couch naps are so important to me that when my wife wanted to buy a new couch, I insisted on lying down on it at the store to make sure it was soft enough for naptime. Who cares about looks? Comfort is what matters! The perfect couch is not too hard nor too soft, made of fabric that is not too scratchy, is long enough to accommodate my six-foot frame, and has pillows that can be placed strategically.

The Art Room

Our "family room" is a bit different from most people's. It's a corner of a big closed-in porch that we have turned into an art corner. It has a big old table and chairs and a cabinet full of art supplies—paints, glue, papers of all sorts, glitter, Popsicle sticks, pipe cleaners, dried flowers, and the like. Sometimes individually and sometimes together, the three of us—mother, father, and daughter—go in there to create something. We make cards, pictures to hang on the walls, and presents for one another and for other relatives. It's a place where each of us can express our creativity. I love to go in there with my three-year-old and finger paint, letting the goopy paint squish through my fingers and seeing what color combinations I can create from the three primary colors. Such a simple pleasure!

Cloth Books

All you need to create this one is an old bedsheet and fabric pens. Cut the sheet into rectangles of uniform size at least 12 inches wide (these will be the pages of the book). Stack the rectangles, matching corners. Fold in half, pin, and sew up the middle to create the book. Draw or write on the pages with fabric pens.

> *Celebrate the happiness that friends are*
> *always giving, make every day a holiday*
> *and celebrate just living!*
> —AMANDA BRADLEY

Sliding Home

The family room in the house I grew up in opened onto a long hallway with hardwood floors. My brother, sister, and I would get into our socks, run, and slide as far as we could down the hall. What fun! When Mom wasn't looking, we'd slide down the banisters as well.

But our favorite sliding game was played with our dog Tira, a Springer spaniel. We would get the small blanket that Tira liked to chew, and get her all whooped up. Then one of us would sit on the blanket and another would go down to the other end of the hall and call Tira. With the blanket edge in her mouth, she would pull us down the hall. Back and forth, back and forth we'd go until we kids all collapsed in giggles and Tira settled down for a well-deserved rest.

Soap Carvings

You and your kids can have fun making soap carvings for presents and use at home.

Just start with a big cake of soap, a potato peeler, a butter knife, and a nail. Use the peeler to carve a design into the soap, the knife to cut off large areas, and the nail to draw designs.

Family Slumber Party

When my in-laws are visiting, we sometimes prepare a late night snack (like ice cream with fruit sauce, or samosas with chai), change into pajamas, open the futon in the family room, bring plenty of extra blankets, spread out on sofas and mattresses, and either watch a scary movie or (my favorite) listen to the stories of my mother- and father-in-law. She tells great ghost stories and family stories; he relates tales of working for the Indian government. We stay up late, then fall asleep all together. It is then that I feel most like a part of their big, warm-hearted family.

> *Perfection consists not in doing extraordinary*
> *things, but in doing ordinary things*
> *extraordinarily well.*
> —ANGELIQUE ARNAULD

Backward Day

My mother was a very inventive soul who believed in having fun without spending money. During summer and winter vacations when we'd run out of things to do, she would wake us up in the morning and declare it "Backward Day." It would be a day in which we would have to do everything backward—say good night when we woke up, walk backward, wear our clothes inside out, eat dessert first and the meal last, say good morning before bed. My brother even used to talk backward: "Park the to go I may?" I could never go that far, but we had fun nonetheless.

> *True delicacy, that most beautiful heart-leaf*
> *of humanity, exhibits itself most*
> *significantly in little things.*
> —MARY BOTHAM HOWITT

Kool Shirts

Here's an activity for a rainy Sunday afternoon, suitable for kids age four and up. Each batch makes one color, but you can do this over and over and make several colors. These are not permanent dyes, so make sure to launder anything dipped in them separately.

> 2 packages of any flavor unsweetened Kool-Aid, depending on what color you want (e.g., orange will make orange dye, cherry will make red dye)
> ½ cup white vinegar
> ½ gallon water
> storage containers with lids

white T shirt
small paintbrush or Q-tip
crayons

Pour the Kool-Aid into a large stainless steel pot with a lid. Stir in vinegar and water. Cover and bring to a boil. Lower heat and simmer for 30 minutes. Allow to cool, and pour into storage containers.

To use, take a clean white T-shirt and paint the dye onto the fabric with a paintbrush or Q-tip. Or draw on the shirt with crayons, then dip the shirt into the dye for a batik look.

Furry Comfort

Home would be pretty darn sterile and lonely if it were not for my cat Roswitha Raguna. I live alone and when I come in the door and she runs to greet me, I feel such love and devotion. When I watch TV, she curls up on the couch with me and I pat her long gray fur. I don't know who enjoys it more—Roswitha or me. And on cold winter nights she's my electric blanket, keeping my feet warm as I sleep. Her rough-tongue kisses, her sweet purr—she makes my house a home.

What's In a Name?

The ASPCA recently polled veterinarians to discover what the top pet names were. They gathered more than 300,000 names; here are the top thirty in order of one to thirty: Max, Sam, Lady, Bear, Smokey, Shadow, Kitty, Molly, Buddy, Brandy, Ginger, Baby, Misty, Missy, Pepper, Jake, Bandit, Tiger, Samantha, Lucky, Muffin, Princess, Maggie, Charlie, Sheba, Rocky, Patches, Tigger, Rusty, and Buster.

*The human heart, at whatever age, opens to
the heart that opens in return.*
—MARIE EDGEWORTH

Kids and Pets

Kids and pets just naturally go together. Well, at least from a very young age, most kids clamor for an animal to be part of the family. They swear up and down that they'll take responsibility, be in charge, that you "won't have to do anything." As any pet-wise parent knows, this is just not true. Kids have no idea how much work a pet is, especially a dog or cat. Before you take the plunge, let them have a taste of the experience. Some wildlife museums have limited-time "rental programs" for hamsters, mice, or guinea pigs so that kids can experience what it's like to care for a pet daily. Or offer to babysit a friend's dog or cat while they're away so your child (and you) can see just what it entails.

Natural Flea Collar

This is filled with pennyroyal, which is said to be a natural flea repellant.

long scraps of cotton fabric
sew-on Velcro
dried pennyroyal

Cut a strip of cotton fabric that is 2½ inches wide and 4 inches longer than your pet's neck is around. Fold lengthwise, right side in, and sew up the long side and one short side. Turn right side out. Sew a 2-inch piece of Velcro on the closed side of the band. Stuff the tube with pennyroyal, leaving about a half-inch unfilled, and fold the unsewn edge under a quarter inch. Close this edge by sewing another piece of Velcro on top, so that the Velcro pieces match up when the collar goes around your pet's neck. Makes 1 collar.

"Stained Glass" Votives

Here's an activity my kids did in first and second grade that really turned out well and is worth sharing.

small baby food jars
tissue paper, different colors
liquid starch
ribbon
tea light candles

Take small baby food jars, wash them thoroughly, and take off the labels. Cut different colors of tissue paper into small squares. Pour liquid starch in a spray bottle; spray starch on a jar and then apply squares of tissue paper all over the outside of the jar until completely covered. Let dry. Tie a ribbon around the neck of the jar, and place a tea light candle inside. When the light shines through, it is quite lovely.

I finally figured out the only reason
to be alive is to enjoy it.
—RITA MAE BROWN

Slowing Down

The first thing I like to do when I come home from work is change into my favorite pair of track pants, T-shirt, and slippers—this marks the transition. Then I love to take a half-hour curled up on the family room sofa under my favorite blanket with a book or long article in hand before interacting with the outside world again. It's the only sure thing that allows me to switch from feeling stressed and tense to relaxed and open.

By Hand

When I was a kid, we never bought presents or cards for family members—we always made them. Even though I am not particularly "handy," I always loved the process of making simple crafts—Play-Doh ornaments dried in the oven, colored bath salts for Grandma, soap with decoupaged angels. As long as it wasn't too hard to do, I was game. One thing we often did for Christmas presents was to make pomanders from oranges. Nothing could be easier—simply stud it with cloves and voilà! Recently I learned that we were only doing half of the project. The other half consists of rolling the orange in a curing mixture so it will last longer and smell better. It is still a wonderful family project—give it a try.

Pomander

4 firm, thin-skinned oranges

large whole cloves

knitting needle, optional

4 ounces cinnamon

2 ounces ground cloves

$\frac{1}{2}$ ounce ground allspice

$\frac{1}{2}$ ounce ground nutmeg

1 ounce powdered orrisroot

large pottery or glass bowl that will hold the oranges

ribbon of your choice

Stud the oranges with cloves—try not to bruise the fruit. If you use a knitting needle to make holes for the cloves, it's easier on the fingers—and the orange. Leave a half-inch space around the circumference of the orange where the ribbon tie will go. Combine the cinnamon, cloves, allspice, nutmeg, and orrisroot in a small bowl. Sprinkle half of the spice mixture into the large bowl. Add the oranges, then sprinkle the remaining spice mixture on top. Store in a cool, dry place. Daily, turn the pomanders and sprinkle with the mixture, until they are hardened—2–5 weeks. Add a ribbon hanger around the circumference of the orange. Makes 4.

Homemade Stickers

If you have kids under the age of twelve, chances are they love stickers. And they can be mighty expensive to purchase. But you can turn any picture you want into a sticker.

Collect appropriate images. Then, in a small cup, mix 2 parts white glue and 1 part vinegar. Use a small paintbrush to brush the mixture on the back of the picture. Let dry 1 hour, then cut, lick, and stick. The advantage to homemade stickers is that kids will have a ball making them!

> *The ornament of a house is the*
> *friends that frequent it.*
> —RALPH WALDO EMERSON

The Play's the Thing

When I was young, whenever my five cousins and I got together for some holiday, after the activities were over (the eggs found, the turkey eaten, the presents opened), the hours would stretch in front of us like the Sahara Desert. What could we do for fun? Inevitably, someone would suggest a performance of some kind: creating a dance routine and lip-synching to *The Sound of Music,* or a gymnastic show where we would throw one another through the air, or a short skit or play.

We would spend hours gathering props and costumes, bossing one another around, and shooing the grown-ups away. Finally, the time would arrive for the show (usually parents telling us we had to pack up and go home in a half-hour), and we'd gather all adults in the vicinity to come and watch us perform. We had such a ball.

Now that I am an adult, my kids and their cousins do the same thing. I think a lot of the pleasure now is in remembering myself at that age, and how much joy I could get out of prancing around thinking I had the voice of Julie Andrews and the dance moves of Fred Astaire.

> *Give happiness and joy to many other people.*
> *There is nothing greater or better than that.*
> —LUDWIG VON BEETHOVEN

A Crawling Maze

When the kids are after me for something to do, I often fall back on an activity I used to do when I was young—make a maze in the family room to crawl through. The construction process is at least as much fun as doing the maze, and certainly takes more time. First, however, you must remove all the breakables—lamps, knick-knacks—from the designated room. Then wind layers of string around and to and from doorknobs, table legs, chairs, and window fixtures to create the supporting structure. Drape the strings with blankets and towels to make the tunnels. Once kids have crawled through a few times and have gotten bored, encourage them to use the structure as a play house and host a tea party.

Helping Hands Apron

Here's an extremely simple project for children to do for a special someone.

Buy an inexpensive plain, white chef's apron. Have your kids put their hands in fabric paint, and press their hands onto the apron in whatever pattern they want. Write "So-and-So's Helping Hands" with a fabric marker, if desired.

Lining the Walls

For years now, I've been lining the walls of the hallway and family room with photos of family and friends. To create visual consistency, I use inexpensive narrow black wooden frames that I buy at an art supply store. Most of the people I'm closest to live far away, and this is the way I bring them near to me. Many days, especially when I'm feeling down, I walk the room, looking at each person, remembering when the photo was taken and thinking of how much he or she means to me.

I count myself in nothing else so happy as in a
soul remembering my good friends.
—WILLIAM SHAKESPEARE

Keeping Memories Alive

There are a number of wonderful ways to display photos inexpensively. Here are some ideas to get you started:

- Photo collages: Collect different-sized pictures in frames from yard sales and flea markets. Throw the pictures away. Cut a poster board the size of the frame for the backdrop, then create a collage with snapshots, gluing the pictures to the poster board, and insert into the frame. Think in themes—birthdays, Christmas over the years, your daughter's volleyball career, vacation shots of you and your husband.

- Purchase inexpensive clear 8-by-10-inch acrylic box frames and have favorite photos blown up to 8-by-10-inch size. Arrange them attractively on the wall.

- Find old window frames without glass. Tack pictures and other mementos on the wall and place the frame over them to create the illusion of looking through a window.

Delights of Decoupage

Have you ever done decoupage? As a teen, I went mad for it for a while. My best achievement was a plaque I made once for my father (who had a very healthy sense of self-esteem) showing a man with his arms outstretched, saying, "I'm the greatest." In case the bug has never bitten you, decoupage is really nothing more than an upgraded version of elementary school cut-and-paste. It's a way of making personalized keepsakes from almost anything—lamp-shades, boxes, trays, table tops—by gluing on a collage of pictures and then coating it with polyurethane until it appears to be embedded in the background. If you have a friend who loves bees, for instance, you can collect images of bees and make her a tea tray. Or an old thrift store chair can be turned into a one-of-a-kind creation by decoupaging the seat and painting the rest in a coordinating color. Before you grab the scissors, however, there are a few basics you should know.

Decoupage Helpful Hints

- Supplies needed: project base (plaque, box, chair, etc.); background paint; images made of paper for collage; spray glue; clear varnish or polyurethane for finish; artist's brushes.

- The surface to be decoupaged must be clean and, if wood or metal, sanded free of paint, dirt, or rust. Wood or metal should then be painted with a base coat of primer and several coats of latex, acrylic, or oil paint.

- Create the collage you want. Remember—the design will look better if it's layered. Fix each piece, beginning with the bottom pieces, with glue and smooth out bubbles or wrinkles as you go.

- Add seven to ten layers of polyurethane or clear varnish, being sure to let it dry completely between coats; drying overnight is best.

Decoupage Supplies

If you're having trouble finding what you need at hobby or craft stores, contact Adventures in Crafts Studio in New York (212-410-9793).

The worst of all possible things is not to live in the physical world.
—WALLACE STEVENS

Are You Game?

A friend of mine, instead of tossing out old board games that have missing pieces, hangs them on the wall of her family room. Scrabble, Monopoly, Risk—she sets up the game as if they were playing it and glues it to the wall. It's quite a conversation piece.

Fun with Fictionary

I generally hate playing games. But recently I was introduced to one that I think is actually fun: fictionary. All you need to play is a few people and a dictionary. One person starts by opening the dictionary and picking a weird word that no one knows. Everyone writes down on a piece of paper a made-up definition; the dictionary holder writes down the correct definition. Then the dictionary holder collects all definitions and reads them aloud and everyone votes for the correct one. If someone guesses correctly, he or she gets three points. If no one guesses the correct one, the dictionary holder gets three points. If your wrong definition is chosen, you get one point. Then the dictionary is passed to the next person.

It's quite hilarious and offers a chance to be very creative. I was playing with friends who made up such believable definitions that I was fooled again and again. I haven't laughed so hard in years.

OUTDOOR SPACES

Anywhere you live, you can find room
for a garden somewhere.

—JAMIE JOBB

The Pleasure of Porches

I've never really trusted a house without a porch. Porchlessness is like a full frontal assault and can seem downright rude in its forwardness—like one of those people who run up and talk so close to you that you can see the little marks on their faces. A porch extends a coy, flirtatious invitation to a house. It doesn't have to be an exact, formal structure of a porch per se—large columns and wide steps are not mandatory. But some semblance of an interim point between the outside and the inside is nice. Stoop, patio, portico, verandah—nomenclature aside, the things that make a porch are the intangible things that transform the mere structure of a house into the uniqueness of a home.

Growing up in the South, our porch was really a carport that not so gracefully stepped down to a patio but, nonetheless, it played the role well enough. It eased the entry into the front door and gave you that polite transitional space. I remember summer evenings on that porch. Warm nights melting into twilight after the yard had been mowed or the laundry taken off the line. The tinkle and clink noises of my mama washing up the last of the dinner dishes, followed by the screen door creak as she came out to sit in her white patio chair. We'd drink sweet tea and watch as the night courted the day into submission. Evening would be dotted by the sparks of lightning bugs that floated to the tune of the cicada trills and frog chirps. We'd talk about people—who was misbehaving, who should've been—until it became so dark that the porch light was circled by a living lampshade of moths and flying beetles. That would signal our retreat into the house, where we'd put away the dishes and make our way to bed, where the insect symphony and the whir of ceiling fans would lull us to sleep in the humid air.

There is something about sun and soil that heals broken bodies and jangled nerves.
—NATURE MAGAZINE

Catching the Rays

I have to confess, my true simple pleasure is sitting in the sun on my patio. I know it's not good for your skin, so I've learned to use mega-sun block. I position the chaise lounge carefully so my full body is exposed, grab a good book, my sun hat, and a frosty glass of ice tea, and stretch out. I pretend I'm lounging on the French Riviera or a beach in Mexico. I have a couple of sun-worshipping friends, and when we are together on our matching chaise lounges, we can talk the afternoon away.

April Showers

My favorite household chore is the yearly spring shower for my indoor plants. I carry them all outside and thoroughly hose them off with water, sometimes hand-washing individual leaves if they are particularly dusty. Then I pluck dead leaves and bulbs, trim brown ends with scissors, and replace old soil with fresh soil if needed. When I return the plants indoors, they sparkle so that I could swear they are thanking me.

Leisurely Fun

Recently some friends invited us to a croquet tournament on a large lawn. We were all supposed to dress in white and arrive at 1 P.M. They served a buffet lunch and then the game began. It was great fun—I hadn't played since I was a kid and accidentally hit the next-door neighbor in the nose with my mallet! Fortunately, there were no injuries, just a leisurely afternoon full of laughter and friendly competition. It so inspired me that I ran out and got a croquet set for my family.

Time for Tracing

One thing my kids and I like to do outside is "sidewalk people." The kids lie down on the driveway, and I trace their bodies with chalk. Then they stand up and use colored chalk to draw in clothes, features, and hair. It's great fun—and it washes off with the garden hose!

By Hand

In the winter I shovel snow. I stand with the snowflakes falling on my bare head, sometimes at two in the morning when the rest of the world is asleep, sometimes at two in the afternoon when the birds are screeching for more seed in their feeder and the boys inside the house are too loud for me. I shovel our entire driveway—knowing we could hire a plow, knowing the snowblower sits idle in the garage, knowing that soon the snow will be two inches deep again.

Water Baby

There is nothing that gives me greater pleasure at home than my hot tub. I have moved three times in the past seven years, and every time, my hot tub comes with me. It's my one true luxury. It's very large and stays hot night and day, so I can go in whenever I want, often twice a day. Sometimes I sit in the quiet, looking up at the stars or watching the winter morning sky slowly brighten. Other times, I put on the jets and feel the pulsations relaxing and soothing my knotted muscles. Sometimes I stay in for so long that I'm dizzy when I get out. If it weren't for my puckered fingers, I think I could stay in all day.

Minimalist Hot Tub

Hot tubs can be expensive and take time to maintain. If you like the idea of bathing outside, consider buying an old-fashioned clawfoot tub (they cost about $100 and fit two people) for outside and run hot and cold water from the house to it. Because you fill and drain it each time (let the water trickle into your garden rather than wasting it), you don't have the hassle and expense of chemicals.

Watering Mindfully

Every year, the sitting area on my deck shrinks as I buy more pots and fill them with summer flowers. I water them slowly, pot by pot. Once in a while, I try to do two things at once— water and talk on the phone. But it's distracting to pay attention to the person at the other end while I'm watching the water flow into the rich brown soil and smiling at the flowers. So, by the beginning of July, I just let the phone ring when I'm watering.

As each plant soaks up the wet nourishment, I stand amidst the air, the smells, and the sounds of life, and all of it helps to slow my world down, quiet my thoughts, and give me time to pause.

> *All of God's pleasures are simple ones: the rapture*
> *of a May morning sunshine; the stream blue*
> *and green, kind words, benevolent acts,*
> *the glow of good humor.*
> —F. W. ROBERTSON

Hanging Out the Wash

On Saturdays I take the sheets and undies outside into the fresh air and hang them up in the sun and wind. No one else is allowed to do this job—I tell them it's because they don't know how to hang out clothes. I feel the early morning sun on my back and listen to quiet sounds as I leave the long week's ragged days behind. I bathe in the morning light under the clothesline and delight in the feeling of air on my skin after being shut up in the office all week. Oh, yes, I have a dryer, but on nice days it sits silent. Placed on the bed, the fragrant sheets from the line beckon a silent welcome after a tiring day.

Water Therapy

When things get tough, I water the lawn and hose down the drive-way. I know this might sound strange, but it's actually very relaxing. Standing outside in whatever I happen to be wearing that day, I water away and think. The water puts me in a trance, and I focus completely. As the grass gets wet, I feel better. As the dirt on the pavement washes away into the gutter, leaving the area clean, I feel in control.

I have been known to stand outside for hours at a time, watering away my worries. I must add, however, that the drought has put a damper on my little ritual. I've had to take up golf as a substitute.

The music of the night insects has been familiar to every generation of men since the earliest humans; it has come down like a Greek chorus chanting around the actors throughout the course of human history.
—EDWIN WAY TEALE

Dining Al Fresco

For the past twenty years, I've lived in Southern California, and what I like best about it, besides no snow, is the opportunity it gives me to eat outside. We have a big picnic table and for almost three-quarters of the year we can have breakfast, lunch, and dinner outside. I love looking at my garden, smelling the air, hearing the birds, and feeling the sun on my skin as I eat. In the summer, we often host large dinner parties outside. I throw a few candles in old bottles of varying heights, and the side yard is transformed into a romantic courtyard. Even when it is too cold for three meals a day in the winter, whenever it is not raining I take my lunch out to the chaise lounge I've positioned in just the right spot to catch the weak winter rays, and enjoy dining out.

Flower Lights

Here's an easy way to decorate your backyard for a summertime evening get-together—or just for yourself.

silk flowers
1 strand of small white indoor/outdoor Christmas lights
$\frac{1}{2}$-inch wide white or gold ribbon
plastic or silk green leaves
hot-glue gun

Pull apart the silk flowers and discard the stems. Take the light strand and push a light through the center of a flower. Continue until all lights are decorated with flowers. Hot-glue the ribbon to an end of the light strand and begin wrapping the chord. As you wrap, hot-glue the leaf stems to the chord and cover the leaf stems with the ribbon.

Sand Candles

These are some of the easiest candles to make yourself. They are great for outdoor barbecues—they actually repel insects—and they look beautiful too—as they burn more and more, the light shines through the sand. As with all candle-making, be aware that wax heated too high can burst into flames. If this happens, turn off the heat and smother with a lid or damp cloth—do not pour water on; that will make it burn more!

damp sand (not too wet, about 1 cup water
   per bucket of sand)
large mixing bowl
smaller bowl, the desired size of candle
wick
paraffin
wax dye if desired
few drops citronella oil
candy thermometer
wicking needle

Pour sand into the large bowl until it's half-full. Tamp down with your fist. Push the smaller bowl into the sand and add sand around to fill in edges. Remove the smaller bowl, being careful not to disturb the remaining hole.

Measure the depth of the hole and cut the wick to fit, plus 1 inch extra. Heat the wax gently in a saucepan, adding the dye if desired and the citronella; mix well when the wax is melted. When the wax reaches 261° F, remove from heat and gently pour a bit into the center of the mold, trickling it over the back of a metal spoon so that the sand doesn't lose its shape. Wait about 5 minutes, as it seeps into the sand. Then add more, making sure the wax is still 261° F.

After about 2 hours, a depression will form in the middle of the mold. Again, heat the wax to 261° F and fill the depression. Push the wicking needle through the center of the well and lower the wick into the hole. Wind the top of the wick around the needle, and place the needle across the sand (so the wick stands upright).

In about 3 hours, the wax will have hardened completely. Remove the candle from the mold. Trim the wick and smooth the base of the candle with an iron on medium heat. Makes 1.

Candle-Making Supplies

Most hobby and craft stores carry everything you need to make candles of all sorts. But if you have trouble finding what you need, contact Barker Enterprises in Seattle (206-244-1870). They have all kinds of supplies, including over 650 shapes of candle molds. Other good sources are Candlechem Co. in Massachusetts (617-986-7541), Pourette Manufacturing in Seattle (800-800-WICK), and Charlotte Hobbys in Quebec (516-247-2590).

> *Ten thousand flowers in spring, the moon in*
> *autumn, a cool breeze in summer, snow in winter.*
> *If your mind isn't clouded by unnecessary things,*
> *this is the best season of your life.*
>
> —WU-MEN

Old-Fashioned Fun

I love the sun, so it is natural for me to celebrate summer solstice, the longest day of the year, with a barbecue bash on my deck for all my friends. I always serve sangria to the adults and lemonade to the kids, make a big vat of potato salad, ask everyone to bring their own food to barbecue, and voilà. We feast and laugh; all of us—kids and grownups—play silly games like Red Rover and Blind Man's Bluff, and we have a grand old time enjoying the first day of summer.

Homemade Water Slide

You can create your very own water slide for a special summer treat. All you need is a patch of lawn, a large sheet of plastic such as a drop cloth, rocks, a garden hose, and a lawn sprinkler. Simply spread the plastic on the lawn and weigh the edges down with rocks. Hook the sprinkler up to the hose and thoroughly wet the plastic. Then turn the kids loose to slip and slide, periodically wetting down the plastic to keep it slippery.

Guardian Angel

I recently moved into a house on a creek and the first day I was there, I discovered that the creek is also home to a great white egret. Sometimes I see it wading, fishing. Other times, I've looked up and it's flying upstream, just past my yard. What a miracle! It seems like my own personal guardian angel, reminding me, as I have a tendency to forget, that there is more to life than money problems, work, and traffic jams.

Nature is pleased with simplicity.
—ISAAC NEWTON

Winged Wonders

I've always loved birds. Perhaps it's because I long to fly. I remember in elementary school making a papier-mâché redwing blackbird that I was inordinately proud of. Every so often over the years, I get it into my head that I am going to learn the names of the birds I see. I know some—like the jays, redtail hawks, robins, sparrows, chickadees, juncos. But I sometimes get an itch to know more. So I buy a book and try to study, to compare the pictures to the birds flitting by my tiny deck. I think I only once learned a new bird.

Another time I thought I would get a tape to help me differentiate between various birdcalls and songs. But then I realized again that it's a lost cause. I just want to enjoy the colors and the songs, the various kinds of flying patterns—swoops, soars, and flits—the comings and goings of different birds throughout the year. All the pleasure goes out of birdwatching for me when I turn it into something intellectual. So these days I am more than satisfied to sit quietly, watch, and listen.

For the Birds

Nothing could be easier than these two treats for the birds in your life. First, make a sunflower seed wreath. Simply take a large, mature sunflower, remove the stalk from the head and cut the center from the head to form a wreath. If you want to get fancy, you can wire on other bird delights—millet, wheat, pecans. Attach a ribbon or wire hanger, and hang on a fence or tree.

For the second treat, cut "cookies" from stale bread using cookie cutters. Poke a small hole at the top of each "ornament." Spread with peanut butter and press into a tray of bird seed. Hang from a tree using yarn threaded through the hole—the birds can use the yarn in building their nests.

> *The very commonplaces of life are components*
> *of its eternal mystery.*
> —GERTRUDE ATHERTON

For Love of Neighbors

I find that the most special aspect of my home is right outside my front door. We are blessed with wonderful neighbors. Although you choose your home for very specific reasons—location, size, price—you usually gamble on who's living next door. At best, we hope that the people around us are tolerable. The joys of good neighbors are countless—generosity that shares resources, concern that brings security, consideration that begets kindness after kindness. Good neighbors deserve celebrating, so consider this an ode to all the wonderful people who share my immediate vicinity.

Outdoor Art

We have a big old picnic table in our backyard and when the weather is good, this is where I send the kids to do their art projects. That way I don't have to worry so much about cleanup.

Natural Dyes

Here are some great colors you can get from plants that commonly grow in yards and gardens.

Beet leaves and roots: pinkish green

Dandelion leaves and roots: yellow

Elderberries: lavender

Goldenrod flowers: yellow-gold

Parsley leaves: light green

Queen Anne's Lace flowers and stalks: yellow

Red onions: red-brown

Spinach leaves: green

Yarrow flowers: light green

Yellow onions: light brown

Simply heat a good quantity in a little water (1 cup of plant material to 2 cups of water). Bring to a boil and simmer for 45 minutes. Remove from heat and allow to cool. Strain into storage containers.

Herbal Stroll

I always grow a variety of common herbs in my garden for the simple pleasure of being able to stroll out whenever I want to and pick just the right amount of basil, thyme, chives, oregano, marjoram, parsley, or cilantro I need when cooking. I love the sense of self-sufficiency and efficiency it always gives me.

> *You only live once—but if you work it right,*
> *once is enough.*
> —JOE E. LOUIS

Daisy Chains

I grew up next to a field where all sorts of wildflowers bloomed—daisies and black-eyed Susans, buttercups and Queen Anne's Lace. One of my favorite things to do on lazy summer afternoons was to collect daisies and make a chain. Sometimes I would wear it in my hair, sometimes festoon the headboard in my bedroom, sometimes offer it as a present to my mother. I still remember how to do it.

Cut the daisies with long (1-foot) stems. You start with 3 blooms on a flat surface—the ground is just fine—staggered at various heights. Braid these together. Then add a fourth daisy to the center of the three and braid into the chain. Continue as long as you have daisies, time, or patience. Tie off the end with a knot.

Auto Fun

My whole family loves to wash the car—well, in hot weather anyway. Even the eighteen-month-old who can't talk yet likes to get into the act, pointing to spots the rest of us have missed. Fortunately, we all like different jobs: my son likes getting the grime off and playing with the hose (getting the parents soaked is a major part of the fun), Dad is happy to dry and then apply the wax, and I love the magic of buffing and polishing, seeing the drab turn to shine. Naturally we end up soaked and filthy, so we finish by stripping down to underwear and washing underneath the hose.

Even if something is left undone, everyone must take time to sit still and watch the leaves turn.
—ELIZABETH LAWRENCE

Batter Up!

One of the great joys of my life is sitting on my deck in the summer twilight with my son and daughter, listening to our hometown baseball team on the radio. Baseball is a sport that is particularly suited to the radio because the pace of the sound mirrors the pace of the game—sometimes lazy and slow, other times excited and fast. When I sit there, I feel a powerful connection to the century-old tradition of listening to the game. The sun sets, the dark creeps around us, and all feels right with the world.

A house, though otherwise beautiful,
yet if it hath no garden is more like
a prison than a house.

—WILLIAM COLES

Reclaiming the Earth

A few years ago my husband and I moved into a house that was obviously not owned by plant lovers. Concrete was the basic outdoor motif, with the few plants that managed to live in the asphalt jungle all in the wrong places—roses in the shade, ferns in the sun, to name just two egregious mistakes. The previous owners didn't have a clue! At first, I wanted to fix it all up right away—it was *so* ugly, and we love to garden. But we really didn't have the time or the money to do a complete overhaul. So I've had to learn the benefits of patience, and of seeing something slowly being transformed in front of my eyes. The first winter, we started a compost pile and put in a rose garden, transplanting the roses we brought with us from our old house. That summer, we planted morning glories to cover the ugly wrought-iron fencing that surrounded the property and, renting a jack hammer, carved out a vegetable garden from the asphalt. Year after year, we did a little bit more. We made some mistakes—things in wrong places that had to be moved again once other things grew—and the yard's still not where we'd like it to be, but overall it has been quite a success. It gives me great pleasure to see how much it's changed already, and I'm grateful for the need to go slow. It puts me more in touch with the rhythm of the natural world, the great wheel of the seasons, 'round and 'round at a stately pace.

Great Gardening Catalogs

I use gardening catalogs to find out about new plants, to get ideas for garden design, and to purchase items local nurseries don't carry. Good general ones include Park Seed (800-845-3369), The Seed Catalog (800-274-7333), and The Cook's Garden (802-824-3400). More specialized ones include

Tomato Growers Supply Company (813-768-1119), Johnny's Selected Seeds (207-437-4301), and my personal favorite, Shepherd's Garden Seeds (on the East Coast, 860-482-3638; on the West Coast, 408-335-6910) which has a wide selection of unusual, easy to grow, disease-resistant vegetables and lots of old-fashioned flower strains.

A wonderful resource for organic gardening items, including fruits, vegetables, and even weed control items, is Gardens Alive! To receive a catalog, call 812-537-8650. Other good sources for organic gardeners are Harmony Farm Supply (707-823-9125; the catalog costs $2) and Peaceful Valley Farm Supply (916-272-4769).

In addition to great nontoxic solutions to pesticides, composting containers, and lots of water-saving and other unique gardening supplies, Gardener's Supply Company (800-863-1700) has wonderfully fun things for green thumbs, including mushroom kits and kits for baking bread in terra cotta pots— my favorite is the Vermont-Grown Kitchen Garden, which delivers an entire garden's worth of top-quality plants to your door. The set contains seventy-one vegetables and twenty-seven herbs, specially selected for performance and flavor. Including three each of three tomato varieties, twelve early and twelve late lettuces, three asparagus, and nine sweet peppers. Also wonderful is White Flower Farm (800-503-9624), which carries seasonal wreaths, unique plants, and other great stuff.

What was Paradise but a Garden?
—WILLIAM COLES

Start 'Em Young

I wanted my kids to love gardening as much as I do. So recently I planted a big "M" and a big "J" (their first initials) in marigolds and filled in between with leaf lettuce. Aside from producing enough lettuce to keep the country's salad bars in heaven, my kids have had an active interest in gardening ever since.

I also plant a lot of herbs, especially highly scented ones, to engage the kids' senses. There are always flowers for them to pick and for friends to take home. I'll never forget the look on my neighbor's face (she's a widow) when my son Matthew gave her a handful of cosmos. Our garden may have many flowers, vegetables, and herbs, but mostly it is full of joy.

To dig one's own spade into one's own earth!
Has life anything better to offer than this?
—BEVERLEY NICHOLS

Gifts for Gardeners

Many catalogs carry great gifts for plant lovers. Here is a listing of the best garden gift catalogs I know:

- Orchids, Etc. (800-525-7510) for plants, fresh flowers, and floral gifts.
- Casual Living (800-843-1881) for great garden furniture and home and outdoor living accouterments.
- Gardener's Eden ([AU: Phone number?]) for garden tools and apparel, landscaping accessories, and live plants and flowers.
- Mountain Farms Inc. (704-628-4709) for dried herbs and flowers.
- Smith & Hawken (800-776-3336) for wonderful plants and tools, fountains, outdoor furniture, pond kits, books, and gardening clothes and accessories.
- Spring Hill Nurseries (800-582-8527) for bonsai, perennials, annuals, ground covers, fruit trees, and gardening supplies.
- Plow & Hearth (800-627-1712) for unique items such as landscape bridges, martin houses, and pond kits as well as furniture and garden supplies.

- Winterthur Museum & Gardens (800-767-0500) for upscale outdoor art, jewelry, garden materials, and home decor accessories.

Worm Farm

Here's an activity to do with little ones.

Search your yard for about ten worms. Fill a 1-gallon glass jar with alternating layers of sand and garden soil until it is almost full, then add compost items such as coffee grounds, banana peels cut into pieces, or old dried leaves. Place the worms on top and cover with a piece of black cloth. Whenever curiosity strikes, remove the cloth for a few minutes and see what the worms are up to. When interest wanes, return worms to the garden.

One day, a couple of million years ago, one of our ancestors was having a snack of saber-toothed tiger steak, when it accidentally fell into the fire. Before he could get it out, it was ruined—all horrible brown, instead of nice and bloody. Nevertheless, since the cave was running low on saber-toothed tiger that week, he decided to eat it anyway. And he liked it! . . . Today, most of us have meals outdoors every chance we get—on porch, patio or lawn.

—GENERAL FOODS
KITCHENS COOKBOOK, 1959

A Year-Round Passion

Barbecuing has become a year-round passion for me. Fortunately I live in a mild climate. Otherwise I would freeze to death or never get the coals going. I mean, I can't imagine trying to light a bunch of briquettes standing in three feet of snow. The worst weather I face takes a sweatshirt and raincoat and an extra trip to the briquette chimney with newspaper to make sure the coals are lit.

I had never thought about barbecuing until my wife insisted on having steaks on her birthday. We had not yet been married for a year. Before that, I had lived in San Francisco, where my roommate and I always had dinner in the apartment. The question of who was to make the meal meant who was going to make the walk to the take-out counter. When I moved in with my wife, she quickly informed me that she considered barbecuing a skill every man had to have. I just had no clue as to how to do it. Thinking it would be easy and being too pig-headed to listen to anyone who knew more than me (read that as my wife), I launched into it wholeheartedly. I did listen to advice to use a chimney as a starter, so there were no lighter fluid accidents. But there were a number of times that included repeated declarations of "Ready!", followed by several trips to the grill to give the food more time to cook. Not to mention the times when everyone knew the food was cooked because you had to crack the charcoal covering to get to the food.

I was having less than stellar success when along came my wife's birthday. I realized the day of reckoning had arrived. It was raining pretty hard that evening, but I wanted to prove to myself that I had the wherewithal to stand in the rain for ten minutes and cook the steak right. A friend had told me to put wood chips on the coals to smoke the meat as it cooked. That and the time I spent patiently getting wet keeping an eye on the meat created a great meal neither of us has forgotten. It was only topped this Thanksgiving when I barbecued a twenty-two-pound turkey. That was the best turkey we've ever had.

Now I'm hooked—I'm out there rain or shine at least once a week. Recently I hit upon adding grapevines to the coals. It gives the meat an incredible flavor that's like nothing else. Maybe there is something to the notion that barbecuing subliminally reminds us of our cave-dwelling days. I do know that it gives me a great deal of satisfaction to do it right.

The Best Barbecue Sauce

The taste for barbecue sauce is very personal. Some like it hot—very hot—and some like it sweet—too sweet for me. Personally, I find the following blend to be just the right compromise, but feel free to experiment in one direction or the other, depending on your preference. It's great on chicken or ribs, and folks in my family also put it on their rice or potatoes in lieu of butter.

1 cup tomato paste

¼ cup vinegar

2 tablespoons sugar

2 tablespoons Worcestershire sauce

1 tablespoon molasses

2 cloves garlic, minced

¼ of a medium onion, minced

salt and pepper to taste

Combine all ingredients and taste. Adjust the sauce to your liking—depending on your preference, it may need more of one thing or another. This is a basic sauce. To make a spicier barbecue sauce, add chili pepper or cayenne pepper to taste. For a south of the border accent, add cumin. For a Polynesian flavor, add minced pineapple. Makes about 1½ cups.

Other Barbecue Delights

Meat and vegetables are not the only barbecue candidates. Here are two great dessert recipes.

Barbecued Bananas

4 bananas

lemon juice to taste

dark brown sugar to taste

butter

Peel bananas. Brush each with lemon juice, sprinkle with sugar, and dot with butter. Wrap tightly in double thick aluminum foil and grill for about 15 minutes, turning frequently. Remove from grill and remove foil. Serves 4.

Caramel Apples

This is an incredibly wonderful barbecue treat—one that each person must make for her or himself! But be careful to let cool before eating—caramel has a tendency to cool slowly.

    4 medium apples
    small bowl melted butter
    small bowl brown sugar
    finely chopped peanuts (optional)

Place each apple on a shish kabob skewer. Hold it over the coals, turning frequently, until the skin can be pulled off. Without removing the apple from the skewer, peel, dip in butter, then dip in brown sugar, covering completely. Hold the skewered apple over the grill and slowly turn until sugar becomes caramelized. Dip in peanuts if desired, and cool completely. Serves 4.

It matters immensely. The slightest sound matters.
The most momentary rhythm matters. You can do
as you please, yet everything matters.
—Wallace Stevens

Preserving Diversity

I sing the praises of heirloom seeds, which are from seeds that have not been hybridized but are direct descendants of plants that in some cases have been around for centuries. I have gardened with the seeds of the past for many years now. It started with orange pepper plant seeds from a fellow gardener. He mentioned in passing that it was an older seed that he had been growing for years, harvesting a bit from each generation for the next year. I grew them that year and was pleasantly surprised at the quality and taste of the pepper. It was a bit thinner-skinned than I was used to but the flavor was wonderful. That's when I discovered the whole world of heirlooms. In some cases, the companies that offer the seeds go searching the world for native flowers and vegetables. They collect them and offer them to gardeners so that the plants will survive if their place of origin is destroyed or the farming there becomes industrialized. (Industrialized agriculture needs a crop that can stand the rough handling of machines. Native and heirloom plants tend to be unable to withstand machine farming.) I like knowing that my little garden patch is helping preserve a bit of the Earth's diversity. The other wonderful thing is that the different varieties of fruits and vegetables each have their own flavors. Unlike grocery store varieties, one type of tomato actually tastes different from another. And that is truly wonderful!

Heirloom and Native Plants

If you are interested in gardening with heirlooms and/or native plants, here are some sources:

- Select Seeds Antique Flowers (860-684-9310).
- Shepherd's Garden Seeds (on the East Coast, 860-482-3638; on the West Coast, 408-335-6910). A great source for heirloom vegetables and plants.
- Seed Savers Exchange (319-382-5990). Since 1975 Seed Savers has distributed over 750,000 heirloom vegetable, fruit, and flower seed samples. The fee for joining the organization is $25 per year.
- Larner Seeds (415-868-9407). Specializes in California Native Plants. $2.50 for a catalog.
- Native Seeds Search (520-622-5561).
- Tomato Growers Supply Co. (941-768-1119). Hundreds of varieties of tomatoes and peppers.

Sandbox Solution

I wanted my toddler to have a sandbox, but I didn't want to spend a lot of money on it. I wasn't sure she would like it, or for how long. I tried making one out of a plastic wading pool. It's perfect! It fills easily with only a few bags of sand (special sandbox sand is available at Home Depot and other hardware stores), and I use a piece of black plastic held down with a few rocks to cover it when it's not in use. (It's important to always cover sandboxes when kids are gone, otherwise neighborhood cats use them as their kitty litter boxes, which can be the source of several terrible illnesses.) In the winter, we simply store the sand and the pool in the garage.

Outdoor Bathing

When the hot days of summer come around, I like to let my kids bathe outside in the wading pool. As it is filling, I squirt some bubble bath under the running hose water, add the toys from the tub, and let the kids play as long as they want. They can play literally for an hour or longer. When they are ready to come out, I simply hose the soap off.

> *There are terrible temptations that it requires*
> *strength, strength and courage to yield to.*
> —OSCAR WILDE

A Family Affair

I love to sit on the porch on hot lazy weekends, not doing much of anything except getting hot. Then I'll suddenly announce to my kids, "Ice cream time!" I'll get the ingredients ready, then enlist them all (by now the neighbor kids have wandered over; perhaps they can smell the sugar) to take a turn with the crank on our old-fashioned ice cream maker. Excitement builds as everyone anticipates the cool, delicious feel of ice cream sliding down their throats, and because there's a crowd, no one has to work too hard to make it happen. I'm always surprised at how much enjoyment we all get out of making it ourselves!

Vanilla Ice Cream

Here is a basic recipe. You can use it as a base for all sorts of other flavors—add ⅓ cup chopped chocolate chips for chocolate chip, ⅓ cup Red-Hots for a Valentine's treat, or ⅓ cup chopped peppermint candy for peppermint (substitute peppermint extract for the vanilla). In each case, add the extras after the final beating.

> 2 eggs plus 2 yolks
> 6 tablespoons sugar
> 1¾ cups milk
> 1 teaspoon vanilla
> 1 cup heavy cream, lightly whipped

Beat the eggs and yolks with the sugar until smooth. In the top of a double boiler, heat the milk until scalding, then add eggs and sugar mix, beating continuously until thickened. Chill. Add the vanilla and fold in the cream. Turn into an ice cream paddler or ice trays. If using a machine, follow instructions. If using ice trays, beat three times at 30 minute intervals while in the freezer, then when it begins to get firm, turn into a chilled bowl and beat well to stop crystals from forming. (This is when you add nuts or candies.) The ice cream will set in about 2 hours. Serves 6.

Cat Stroll

It's early morning and I'm out doing a little weeding and watering accompanied by my three cats. They love to play "big kitty in the jungle" when I'm out in the yard, following me and my hose around. Callahan proudly brings me a bunch of sourgrass I've just pulled, the way other cats bring their owners dead mice. I tell him dogs have peed on it, but that doesn't diminish his pleasure. The sun shines, the cats stalk, and all is right in my world.

INDEX

OTHER SIMPLE PLEASURES BOOKS
FROM CONARI PRESS

Simple Pleasure: Soothing Suggestions and
Small Comforts for Living Well Year Round

Simple Pleasures of the Garden: Stories, Recipies,
and Crafts from the Abundant Earth

Simple Pleasures for the Holidays: A Treasury of Stories
and Suggestions for Creating Meaningful Celebrations

Conari Press, established in 1987, publishes books on topics
ranging from psychology, spirituality, and women's history to
sexuality, parenting, and personal growth. Our main goal is
to publish quality books that will make a difference in
people's lives—both how we feel about ourselves
and how we relate to one another.

Our readers are our most important resource,
and we value your input, suggestions, and ideas.
We'd love to hear from you—after all,
we are publishing books for you!

To request our latest book catalog, or to
be added to our mailing list, please contact:

CONARI PRESS
2550 Ninth Street, Suite 101
Berkeley, California 94710-2551
800-685-9595   510-649-7175
fax: 510-649-7190
e-mail: Conari@conari.com
www.conari.com